The Spirit-Filled Life

Mónica E. Mastronardi de Fernández

Church of the Nazarene
Mesoamerica Region

·DISCIPLESHIP·
abcde
growth in holiness

Level C - Growth in Holiness
Youth/Adults

Title: The Spirit-Filled Life

Book of "Discipleship ABCDE"
Level C - Growth in Holiness
Series: Filled with the Spirit
Study Guide for Youth/Adults

Author: Mónica Mastronardi de Fernández
Editor: Dra. Mónica Mastronardi de Fernández
Reviewers: Jerald Rice, Dorothy Bullón, Rubén E. Fernández, Samuel Pérez.

With the collaboration of:
BSc. Joel Poveda (lessons 4,5,6,8)
Dr. Rubén E. Fernández (lesson 12).

Material produced by: Discipleship Ministries, Church of the Nazarene, Mesoamerica Region
Discipleship Ministries www.SDMIresources.mesoamericaregion.org
Discipleship@mesoamericaregion.org

Copyright © 2017 - Rights reserved

ISBN: 978-1-63580-069-2

All quotations are taken from New International Version (NIV) unless otherwise stated.

Translated from Spanish to English by Dr. Dorothy Bullón

Design: Juan Manuel Fernández.Ga (www.juanfernandez.ga)
Front cover image by Mathew Yeo
Cover Images are used with permission under the license of Common Property (Abstracto/Quito)

Printed in the U.S.A

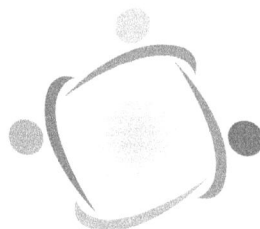

Mesoamerica Region

Table of Contents

Presentation

Discipleship ABCDE

How to use this book

Lesson 1 - Who are we and where did we come from? *10*

Lesson 2 - The destructive power of sin *20*

Lesson 3 - The role of the Holy Spirit in our salvation *30*

Lesson 4 - The human part of salvation *42*

Lesson 5 - Salvation: a transformative experience *52*

Lesson 6 - Sinful attitudes that need to be cleansed *62*

Lesson 7 - Natural, carnal or spiritual? *74*

Lesson 8 - A long and dangerous childhood *86*

Lesson 9 - How to receive the fullness of the Spirit of love *98*

Lesson 10 - From Simon to Peter: Internal Changes Resulting from the fullness of the Spirit ...*110*

Lesson 11 - Perfect Love: Lifestyle of the Spirit-filled Christian ...*122*

Lesson 12 - Common errors about the fullness of the Spirit ...*132*

Lesson 13 - Setting goals for my spiritual life ...*142*

Presentation

The Christian's life is a continuous walk in the process of discipleship, in which our whole being is being transformed to become like Jesus Christ through the Holy Spirit's work in us. All of us who have been "born again" need to participate in this process of formation so that we can become mature and holy Christians in all areas of our lives.

This volume titled: **The Spirit-Filled Life** is the first of a three-volume series that completes the basic studies for level C of the ABCDE Discipleship Plan of the Church of the Nazarene in the Mesoamerica Region. The series is called: **Filled with the Spirit** and covers 9 months of studies. Each book contains 13 discipleship lessons focused on the consolidation and growth needs of people who have recently been incorporated into local church membership.

These lessons have been written with the thoughtful discipler/teacher in mind, and offers guidelines about how the teacher should instruct the group of new members in such a way that the class is interesting, dynamic and applicable to their lives. These books present the doctrine and practice of the life of holiness in simple practical language, and at the same time connect with the ideas of the contemporary world. The holy life is studied emphasizing:

A) The natural and progressive changes that are produced in the Christian, as a result of the action of the Holy Spirit in one's life; changes that are observable not only by oneself, but by all those around him or her.

B) The life full of the love of God as an indispensable requirement to serve the Lord and our fellow man.

C) The progressive and total transformation of the life of believers as we become more and more like Jesus Christ.

Each lesson presents a new opportunity for God to continue to work and transform each disciple so that we all might become more like Jesus in the way we think, in our emotions, and lifestyle, through bible studies, examples and illustrations, self-assessment exercises, reflection, as well as the opportunity to set new goals for spiritual growth.

It is my prayer that these lessons will help the members of our churches to understand and live more in the holy lifestyle of our beloved Savior, Jesus Christ.

Rev. Monte Cyr
Discipleship Ministries Coordinator
Mesoamerica Region

What is Discipleship ABCDE?

In the Church of the Nazarene, we believe that making disciples in the image of Christ in the nations is the foundation of the mission of the Church and the primary responsibility of the leadership (Ephesians 4:7-16). The work of discipleship is continuous and dynamic, that is to say, the disciple is never to cease growing more like the Lord. This process of growth, when it is healthy, occurs in all dimensions: as individuals (spiritual growth), in the corporate dimension (becoming part of the congregation), as well as in holiness of life (progressively becoming more like Jesus Christ), as well as in a life invested in service to God and others.

The ABCDE Discipleship Plan has been designed to contribute to the comprehensive formation of members of the churches of the Nazarene in the Mesoamerica Region. We have published materials to cover all discipleship levels. The three books in the **Filled With the Spirit** series correspond to the basic series for Level C, and have been designed for those who have gone through previous levels of discipleship with **New Life in Christ** materials and **Keys to Abundant Christian Living** (Level B1 and B2), and have been incorporated into church membership.

The books of the series **Filled With the Spirit** are intended to guide the new member of the church to become like Jesus Christ. As each person advances in the study of these materials, he or she will be discovering those areas of their lives that Jesus Christ wants to transform, so that the Holy Spirit of love can fill their whole being. The Spirit-filled life is the indispensable prerequisite to enable every son or daughter of God to realize the special plan that God has for his/her life.

•Discipleship•
abcde
Church of the Nazarene

Dr. Mónica Mastronardi de Fernández
General Editor ABCDE Discipleship
Church of the Nazarene - Mesoamerica Region

·DISCIPLESHIP·
abcde
church of the nazarene

Level A | Approach

Evangelism.

Level B | Baptism and Membership

Discipleship for New Believers.

Level C | Continued Growth

"Filled With the Spirit" Discipleship.

Level D
Ministry Development

School of Leadership.

Level D
Professional Development

Specialized Training by
Theological Institutions.

Level E | Education for Life and Service

Wholistic Growth in Christlikeness.

How to use this Book

This book belongs to a series of three volumes on the theme "Filled With the Spirit." The books are designed to be studied in the following order:

1. The Spirit-filled Life

2. The Mind Refocused on Christ

3. The Fruit-filled Life

The purpose of this series is to help the members of the Churches of the Nazarene get to know the biblical teaching on the holy life and to put what they are learning into practice in their daily lives in order to grow in their likeness of Jesus Christ.

How much time is needed to cover the study of the book?

Each book contains 13 lessons. If you guide them to study one lesson per week, the entire study will last three months. Sometimes groups prefer to go slower and spend two weeks studying each lesson. In that case, the study of the book will take 26 weeks (about six months). Remember that the goal of discipleship is not about rushing through to complete a book, but that group members might grow in the likeness of Jesus Christ. And in order to grow, they need to study, understand, and apply these new teachings to their lives. So planning the time for the study of each lesson in advance is very important to ensure the disciples' progressive learning.

By their didactic design, the books can be used in different modalities; either for one-on-one discipleship, in small groups or in classes of more people.

What do the lessons contain?

Each lesson contains the following:

- Objectives: formulation of the learning goals that the students are expected to achieve at the end of the study of each lesson.

- Resources: ideas are included to illustrate and make learning more interesting.

- Introduction: the subject of study is introduced in an interesting way to awaken the interest and participation of students.

- Bible study: this is the most extensive section since it is the development of the contents of the lesson. These lessons have been written with the book as a teaching agent in mind, so its content is expressed in dynamic, simple language and makes connection with the ideas of the contemporary world. This section includes notes to the teacher about student participation in lesson development (Bible reading, questions, exercises from the Activity Worksheet).

- Summary of the main teaching of the passages studied: at the end of the lesson a small summary is provided. This summary is very useful to use at the end of the class as a closing point and/or the beginning of the next session to remember the topics discussed.

- Definition of Key Terms: This section is intended to clarify or broaden the meaning of some of the terms contained in the lesson.

- Activity Worksheets: These pages can be found and copied for the students, although ideally each student should have their own copy of the study booklet. As the lesson progresses, both individual and group learning activities related to the topic will be included.

- Recommended Readings: At the end of the Activity Worksheets, there are bible readings relative to the topics studied. Both teacher and students are encouraged to use these verses in their devotions during the week.

What is the role of the student?

The student is responsible for:

1. Acquiring the book and studying each lesson before each class. This is recommended, depending on the possibilities of each church.

2. Attend classes promptly.

3. Participate in class activities by completing the Activity Worksheets.

4. Apply the teachings of the Bible to their daily lives.

What is the role of the teacher?

1. Prepare the class session beforehand, studying the content of the lesson and scheduling the use of class time. The teacher needs to study the lesson with a Bible and a dictionary available for consultation. Pay attention to the vocabulary used in the lessons, and explain in simple words what might be difficult for the students to understand.

2. The teacher should allow the Holy Spirit to transform his/her own life and put into practice any new teaching, in order to be an example to the students.

3. Pray every day so that the objectives of each lesson becomes a reality in the lives of the disciples. Pray for the specific needs of each one of them.

4. Bring extra copies of the Activity Worksheet when students do not have a copy of the book. Complete the activities to become familiar with the exercises.

5. Prepare the teaching resources well in advance.

6. Connect with disciples outside of class. These lessons are intended to enable people to have transforming experiences which will help them to become more like Christ. Share with them and encourage them to apply to their lives what they are learning, and make sure they know that you are there to help them.

How to teach a class

The lesson should last from between 90 to 120 minutes depending on the number of students and their participation. It is recommended that students read the lesson in advance so that they will have more time in class for discussion and application of the teachings.

In the course of the lesson, directions for the activities in which the students participate are included, such as Bible readings, discussion questions, or exercises to complete in the Activity Worksheet.

Whether you choose to study one lesson per week or one lesson in two weeks, we recommend that you distribute the time as follows (for 90 minutes of class):

- 5 minutes: welcome, review the theme and main points from the previous lesson, and prayer together.
- 10 minutes: introduction to the lesson topic.
- 60 minutes: lesson development. Use visual aids such as blackboard, graphics, drawings, objects, pictures, among others, and encourage student participation through questions or assigning students to take part in the lesson, etc.
- 10 minutes: share testimonies and a time of prayer for the issues raised in the lesson (challenges, personal situations, problems, goals, gratitude, among others).
- 5 minutes: announcements and farewell.

Who are we and for Whom do we live?

Lesson 1

Learning goals:

That the students...

- Discover the purpose for which the Creator has given them life.

- Recognize that they are a special creation of God, with valuable gifts to use in His work in this world.

- To become aware that the life of holiness is the "natural" lifestyle for which we were created, and sin is an acquired problem and should not be considered normal for Christians.

- Set goals to reorder their lives according to God's purposes.

Resources

- Find 16 pictures of animals and younger versions of the same animals. Include some human adults and some children. You could include several breeds of dogs. Glue the adult on one piece of paper and the young one on another piece of paper. You can also include some loose pictures, for example, only a puppy or only a father so that some are without a match.

Introduction

In this quarter, we're going to talk about the purpose for which each of us was created and saved by Jesus. In this lesson, we'll begin by studying the biblical passages that speak about the history of the origins of the human race in order to discover why God has given us life. We'll find out that we've a valuable mission to carry out in this life for God and with our fellow men.

Because many people ignore or have forgotten this purpose, God through His Word reveals to us this wonderful plan for our life and calls us to follow it.

Bible Study

1. WE WERE CREATED IN THE LIKENESS OF GOD

▌▌▌ Begin the study by asking a student to read Genesis 1:26-27. ▌▌▌

These two verses tell us that human beings are not the result of a genetic accident; our life did not come into existence as the fruit of thousands of years of natural evolution, but we're a special creation of God. He said *"Let us make mankind."*

The most important teaching comes twice in verse 27 *"So God created mankind in his own image, in the image of God he created them; male and female he created them."*

▌▌▌ Distribute the pictures of adults and their offspring on a table or on the floor. Have students join each puppy or child with their parents, letting them be guided by physical similarities. Then ask: How did we realize which children belonged to their parent? The answer will be: because they resembled each other. Conclude the exercise by saying, "In the same way the Bible says that God created us in His image." ▌▌▌

·· Do group activity No. 1 on the Activity Worksheet.

Veteran missionary Wesley Duewel says , "We may never fully understand what it means to be made in the image of God until we meet Jesus in heaven." Through this image God has imprinted his mark on each one of us. Without that stamp we would be nothing but dust of the earth. To be in the image of God is what gives us our identity as members of the human family, whose genealogical tree has its origin in the Creator. This likeness of God is present in every child born in this world, and even though it has been spoiled by sin, we can still appreciate it.

Some of these special abilities that God has shared with us are the freedom to choose, the power to understand intellectually, the ability to communicate with others, to share our desires,

---

[1] Wesley L. Duewel *God offers you his great salvation.* Nappanee, Indiana: Evangel Publishing House, 2000. p. 20.

our dreams and our emotions. This set of characteristics that God has given us is known as the "natural image."

·····················○ **Do group activity No. 2 on the work sheet.**

God created us as spiritual beings.

The word "spirit" means "breath of God that gives life" (Genesis 2:7, Job 33:4, Ezekiel 37:9).

When God formed man, he made him from the dust of the earth, a material that was not special. What made the great difference was "the breath of life" of God. This was what set us apart from all other things and created beings. God has placed in us his "spirit".

Humans are beings of a spiritual nature. It's the spirit that keeps us alive. Without it we're inert matter. What happens to people when they die? The spirit leaves them and their body has no life … soon it becomes dust … What keeps us alive then is our spirit.

God took the decision to create us as spiritual beings, with physical bodies and with human natures. This spirit enables us to live eternally, beyond physical death. In this sense, we're like angels, who were created before heaven, earth, and human beings (Genesis 1: 1, Job 38: 4-7). The angels were created holy and live in perfect fellowship and loving obedience to God. Angels don't have a physical body like ours.

Hence the value of human beings doesn't reside in their intellectual capacity or abilities to do great work; but in that life that God himself gave them, as His Spirit breathed on them.

We've been made by God with an "empty space" that can only be fully filled by the Holy Spirit of God. The permanence of God's Spirit in us is what will allow us to have a perfect and harmonious relationship with God.

We were created without sin just as God is Holy

The image of God in us goes further; God shared with us his moral attributes. This means that we were made with the ability to reproduce the character of God in our life, or to be as He is.

·····················○ **Ask the group to do Activity no. 3 on the Activity Worksheet.**

God's essence shared with us humans includes his holy character, that is, that we were created with the capacity to live in holiness. We were designed to be holy and all that we are comes from a holy God. God hasn't created anything that's contrary to his own holy nature.

We were created with the need to have friendship and fellowship with God

The relationship of our first parents (Adam and Eve) to God was perfect. What made this fellowship with the Creator possible was the sanctity and purity in which they lived. The first couple knew God face to face and talked with Him.

But because of sin, this relationship was interrupted. The only way by which this lost relationship can be recovered is through the work of Jesus, our only and sufficient Savior. Jesus is the way to the Father, the only one who can restore us to fellowship with God (John 14: 6-7).

⬦ **Complete activity 4 on the Activity Worksheet.**

We were created with freedom to make decisions.

God created the angels with free will. Later he created man and woman with the power to choose freely. Unfortunately, we human beings have abused this freedom and instead of using it to obey God, we've chosen to do the opposite of His will, committing acts of sin and allowing disobedience to take root in our heart and become the engine of our will. God did not ignore this, but even knowing that man and woman could betray his love and trust, he took the risk and created us with free will.

Our limited mind cannot easily understand how wonderful this freedom is that has been given to us, and the glory that it brings to our God, nor the consequences in eternal blessings that moves our lives and those of all humanity when a person decides to choose to live in perfect obedience to the will of God.

Yes, God made us with the possibility of sinning, but He also made us able to accept His offer of salvation in Jesus Christ, who has given us complete freedom from the dominion of sin.

2. EVERY HUMAN LIFE IS VALUABLE BECAUSE IT HAS A HOLY PURPOSE

Have you ever heard this complaint from your children? "Dad, I'm bored ..." Generally, parents begin to give suggestions of some things in which their children could be useful, like mowing the lawn, sweeping the kitchen, helping the little brother with homework, washing the family car ... but the common response we get from them is: "But that's boring." Are children programmed to be bored? No, in reality what happens to them is the most natural thing: they want to invest their time in something that really matters to them; in something they value ... Are we not just like them? Why are we like this?

The answer is found in chapter 1 of Genesis.

We were made to work

What did God charge Adam and Eve in Genesis 1:28 and 2:15 to do? God's first commandment to them was to do a great and very important work: to fill the earth, to govern it and to care for it under God's supervision! This commission was given by God with His blessing. Both mandates were given before sin entered into the hearts of human beings. Already in the garden, Adam and Eve had work to do and had full happiness by dedicating their lives to a good, valuable and profitable purpose, not only for themselves but for all living beings.

So, it's not right to think that work is a punishment that God gave us for sin. Nothing can be further from the truth revealed in the Bible.

When God made us "in His image", He did it so that we could be "responsible for" the whole of creation, so that the Creator could share His work with us. In Genesis 1:26, we see this unity inseparable, *"... so that they may rule over the fish in the sea and the birds in the sky, over the livestock and all the wild animals ..."* In this first chapter of Genesis, we're shown God as a worker: He labored 6 days and on the last one, he rested, contemplating the good work that he had done. That's what the reformer Ulrich Zwingli (1484-1531) stated, " There's nothing in the universe as equal to God the worker." So the Father has given us this great privilege of being workers like Him. We all have work to do in this world created by God. It's interesting to note also that the founders of the Church of the Nazarene chose that name because "it symbolized the humble and laborious mission of Jesus Christ."

Work, far from being a punishment for sin, is a gift, a gift that God has given us. Work is fundamental to our human nature. The word that best describes the job responsibility that God has assigned to human beings is "steward." This isn't a word that we use much today, but it's the one that best describes the function that has been entrusted to us. A steward is someone to whom the owner has entrusted to take care of his possessions. In order to carry out this responsibility, God has given each one of us special abilities (talents and gifts), and we've been given a "part" of the Creator's property so that we can take care of it in the best way we can, as long as our life lasts.

We sometimes think that what we have is ours, and that we can give a part of it to God. People are also often valued for what they have. If this were true in the eyes of God, we would have no value, because a steward doesn't own what he manages. Psalm 24:1 says, *"The earth is the Lord's, and everything in it, the world, and all who live in it."* This means that EVERYTHING is His - the rocks, the plants, the ants, the water, including our life, time, our stuff, our capacities, our professions or trades, our bank account, our children, 100% of everything we are, what we do, what we have and even what we'll have in the future.

At the same time, however, the Bible teaches us that the value of human life doesn't reside in the stuff we possess, but in how we serve God as stewards in the task assigned to us. How much is our life worth then? The psalmist sums it up in Psalm 8:5-6, 9: *"You have made them a little lower than the angels and crowned them with glory and honor. You made them rulers over the works of your hands; you put everything under their feet ... Lord, our Lord, how majestic is your name in all the earth!"*

God appointed Adam and Eve as administrators with the duty to give loving and responsible care of all that God had made. In this sense, it's our responsibility as people to "look after" and "care for" God's creation, keeping it alive, healthy and multiplying, giving glory to the Creator and showing His greatness and benevolence. The good steward does his work in the same way and with the same love that God would do in his place

We were created to love

A person can work hard and not really enjoy what he does. For some people, work becomes a duty, a responsibility. This can happen because they work on something that is not really their vocation. But even people who work in their vocations can become tired and feel like slaves of that task because they lack something fundamental: love. When there is no love, any work becomes tedious and bitter. Any task loses its value when it is not done because of love.

In the first place, we were created to love God. God loves us and He has created us with the capacity to respond to that love. We show our love for God when we worship Him, and express our

---

[2] Cited in *The Service to God*, Ben Patterson, Miami: Vida, 1994. p. 11.

[3] Cited in *The History of the Nazarenes*, Timothy L. Smith, Kansas City: NPH. p.128.

love to Him with songs, prayers, and doing things that show our appreciation. When we're close to God, we give and receive of His love, and that love affects everything that we do, and our work becomes impregnated with the love of God.

We've been created to serve one another in love. In the passage from Matthew 25:37-40, Jesus taught that we cannot say that we serve God and at the same time mistreat our fellow man. Such a fact is inconceivable, for the image of God is also in our neighbor, so we would be treating God himself badly. Serving others with our work is part of our stewardship.

Jesus himself gave us an example of this by serving us by dying on the cross in our place, and thus suffering for us the punishment we deserved for our sin. Colossians 1:15 says, *"The Son is the image of the invisible God, the firstborn over all creation."* In the original this phrase means "an exact representation," someone in whom God can be seen as He is. In the same way, God wants us to be able to serve people by demonstrating His infinite and holy love.

....................................o **Ask the students to complete Activity 5.**

We were created to serve and worship

In the Bible, the same word is used to refer to work (or service) and worship. This word is "liturgy" and is used to refer to what we do for the Lord in the church and the service we provide with our work in everyday occupations.

Both are ways of working and both must give an account to God. The interesting thing is that one of these occupations ends with physical death, but the other will continue to exercise it for all eternity ... Guess which?

In Revelation 4:8 we're allowed to look at what our life will be like in eternity: we'll be worshiping. When we worship God, we're setting a foot in eternity. Eternity fills us with holy love and hope, and must be transmitted in everything we do, even in the smallest detail of any work.

Whether we worship in our room, the office, at church, or in any other place, we get in touch with the God of Life. Yes, the God who has given us being, has made us in his image, gifted us with talents and gifts, filled us with dignity by sharing his creative work with us and given us the insatiable need to enjoy his company and friendship.

....................................o **Ask the students to complete activity 6.**

These abilities to work with joy, to love God and our fellow human beings, and to worship God with our whole being have been deeply affected by sin. That's why in our day human tendency is to disobey more than to obey the Creator. As we'll see in the next lessons, only through the work of Jesus can we recover the true meaning of our existence.

Definition of key terms

- **Adam:** the first man created by God, but at the same time, he is representative of all created humanity. In addition to being the proper name of the first person made in the likeness of his Creator, he represents "humanity."

- **Holiness:** Supreme goodness, absence of evil. It's the opposite of imperfection, of sin, of corruption. It's an attribute of God whose moral purity is perfect. The first humans were created holy as God is holy. They had never sinned or seen evil in other people. This original holiness has been lost, and now we can only be holy if we're cleansed by the blood of Jesus Christ and filled with the Holy Spirit.

- **"Fellowship" / "communion"**: This word in its biblical roots means, "to be part of something" or "to belong to something." We use this word to express that we're part of God or belong to God and that God is part of us.

- **Ministry:** basically related to the "service" that the believer gives to God. Ministry can be service we give to God or a specific field of labor in the Body of Christ, for the purpose of blessing our neighbor.

- **Free will:** the ability that God has given us to make decisions about how we think, speak and act, and how we take control of our own destiny.

- **Steward:** Someone who has been entrusted with the property of another person to administer in the way that most benefits the owner.

Summary

Human beings were created in the image of God. We're not the result of chance or evolution. God has stamped his mark, his seal on each one of us. We're works of art signed by the Creator of the universe, unique and unequaled, created in His image and likeness, that is: with free will, intelligence, ability to communicate and holy. We were created to worship God and serve our fellow men, working on God's purposes with love and joy.

Although this image of God in man has deteriorated because of sin, and humans have deviated from the will of God, there is hope in Jesus Christ by which that image of the holy God can be restored in each person.

Activity Worksheet

ACTIVITY 1
Respond to the following questions based on Genesis 1:26-31; 2:7.

1. According to Genesis 1 and 2, is there any other living creature or thing created besides human beings that was made by God in His image?

_____

_____

2. What is the difference between being "like" and being "equal"?

_____

_____

3. Did God have any plan in mind when He created man and woman with respect to what their specific role would be in creation?

_____

_____

4. What did God do after finishing His work at creation, according to Genesis 1:28? What does this say about how much God values us?

_____

_____

ACTIVITY 2
Sort the following list into two columns. In the first column place the characteristics which are unique to people and in the second, the characteristics of the whole creation of God.

TALKING, GROWING, CHEERING, DESIGNING, DYING, COMPASSIONATE, BREATHING, CONVERSING, SADNESS, MOVING, APPRECIATING BEAUTY, EATING, BREEDING, LOVING, SICKNESS, RUNNING, SLEEPING, REJOICING.

Only for people		All creation	
_____	_____	_____	_____
_____	_____	_____	_____
_____	_____	_____	_____
_____	_____	_____	_____
_____	_____	_____	_____

ACTIVITY 3
What is the moral quality of God that He wants to reproduce in us according to Leviticus 11:44-45 and Exodus 19:5-6?

_____

_____

ACTIVITY 4
Mention some things you can do this week to strengthen your "fellowship with God."

_____

_____

_____

_____

ACTIVITY 5.
According to what you have learned in this lesson about the purpose of human life, mark with a tick the correct answers:

What is work?

__ A curse that man must suffer for his disobedience to God

__ Part of the blessing that God has given to the human beings who were created in His image

__ To collaborate with God as the Creator and sustainer of life

What gives people value?

__ That they were made originally in the image of the Creator

__ Material possessions

__ Special abilities and talents

__ Faithful work done for God.

A good steward is:

__ Someone who looks after his own things

__ Someone who makes sure he/she takes advantage of others

__ One that takes care of the assets of another increasing their value.

When does work become a curse or a burden?

__ When it's done out of love

__ When it's done for selfish motives

__ When it benefits other people

__ When it's done as a duty

Activity Worksheet - Lesson 1

ACTIVITY 6.
Complete the following.

1. Mention some qualities, skills or talents that God has given you as His steward.

_____

_____

2. What changes would you like to make this week with regard to how you do things and how you serve God and others?

In your relationship with God: _____

With your brothers and sisters in the church: _____

With your family: _____

With those with whom you work or study: _____

Pray in pairs, one for the other, putting your goals in the hands
of the Lord and asking for his help to achieve them.

RECOMMENDED READINGS

- *Psalm 8*
- *Psalm 100*
- *Luke 11:42-48*
- *Colossians 1:15-23*
- *1 Peter 1:13-16*

The Destructive Power of Sin
Lesson 2

Learning goals:

That the students ...

- Know that the nature of sin is twofold: an action and a condition.
- Understand that sin has an expansive and destructive power that degrades people, corrupts society, and brings death to the whole of God's creation
- Identify with God's repudiation of sin and His purpose to banish it from the lives of His children.

Resources

- A medium size mirror which allows you to see the whole face. Mud or chalk mixed with water that will serve to dirty the mirror

Introduction

||| Show the students the clean mirror and ask them "What is a mirror for?" (They will respond that it allows us to see ourselves as we are). |||

True, mirrors are created to give us a real picture of how we see ourselves. Many would like the mirror to show us younger, thinner, with more hair, etc.; but a real mirror was not made to lie.

We've studied in the previous lesson that God created us in His image, that is, as mirrors that reflects who He is. This is not a physical image, because God is Spirit and has no flesh and blood or body like us. It refers to how God is in his character.

||| Ask the class: "Do you believe that human beings today are the reflection of the holy character of God?" Now take the mirror and cover it with mud ... and then have the students look at it. Ask them: "What prevents the mirror from reflecting its image?" (Mud, dirt ...) How does the image look? (Deteriorated, blurred, stained ...) In the same way, sin is what prevents us from being able to reflect the full image of God in our lives. |||

In this lesson, we'll see what the Bible tells us about the origin of sin and its destructive power over people's lives.

Bible Study

1. WHAT IS SIN?

The word "sin" (Greek *amartía*) means to miss the target. The idea this term conveys is to take the wrong path or route.

To describe sin according to the teaching of the Word, we must define it in two dimensions.

a. The sin we commit: every thought, act or word that's against the law and the will of God. In this sense, committing sin is an act of voluntary rebellion and disobedience to the known laws of God. When we sin, we're wandering from the path of perfection for which our Father God has created us.

b. The sin we inherited: this is a condition or state that dwells in the heart of every human being and separates us from the holiness of God. This "seed of sin" has been transmitted to us from our first parents, Adam and Eve, to the whole human race. This sin as a state motivates people to commit acts of sin and makes them desire evil (Romans 7:8). The Bible warns us that this "seed of wickedness" is present in every child that's born, and unless we give our lives to Christ, sin will grow and reign over our lives (Romans 6:12).

..................................○ **Ask the students to complete Activity 1.**

2. WHAT IS THE ORIGIN OF SIN?

Just as light is the opposite of darkness, sin is the opposite of holiness. The Bible says in 1 John 1:5, 3:5 that no darkness or sin comes from God. God is one hundred percent holy all the time. His holiness doesn't vary, but is eternal and infinitely perfect. That's why we can safely affirm that sin doesn't come from God. It was never in His mind or heart to create sin, or create a world where sin existed. Everything that He has created is made in harmony with Him and has its origin in His very holy nature. That's why the Bible says that God doesn't tempt anyone (James 1:13).

Sin has its origin in Satan. The Bible says that Satan has power to direct the minds and hearts of human beings to oppose God's plans. That's why Jesus rebuked Peter when Satan had "filled his head" with twisted ideas.

Who is Satan? The Bible doesn't give us much information about the origin of Satan, since it's more concerned with guiding us on the path of salvation. It tells us that Satan was one of the chief angels created by God (Job 1:6). Ezekiel 28:12-17 and Isaiah 14:12-15 say that the kings of Tire and Babylon were allowed to be used by Satan. In the story, the history of these kings mingles with the story of the origin of Satan: how an angel in the service of God allowed pride to come in and became an enemy of God (1 Timothy 3:6; 14:13, 14). When Satan rebelled against God, he lost his place in heaven by the throne of God, and convinced other angels to follow him. The Apostle Paul refers to them as the spiritual forces of evil (Ephesians 6:12).

But we must be careful not to match Satan up with God. God is Almighty, Satan has limited power; God knows everything, Satan's knowledge is limited, God is everywhere, in unlimited space, Satan is limited to one place at a time. That's why he is forced to operate through the demons that obtain information for him and obey his will.

The teaching we have about the Devil and his action in the Bible comes largely from the teachings of Jesus. To stay away from the influence of Satan, we must know the strategies Satan uses to keep us from the will of God. Jesus taught that Satan is the father of all lies (John 8:44). He's the one who has taught human beings to lie and deceive. He's also the origin of hatred and everything that's opposed to love and purity. He uses all his wiles against God, against his church and against human beings. His purpose is to destroy God's plans and steal the glory that belongs to God alone.

Sin entered the human race when Satan induced Eve and Adam to let pride enter their hearts and disobey the will of God (Genesis 3:1-6). However, we're glad to say that God didn't abandon us, nor destroy us.

Satan's tactics haven't changed; he deceives human beings into putting their selfish will above the will of God. People believe that they exercise their freedom by living in sin, ignoring that they have actually fallen into the trap of Satan and become slaves of sin.

..................................○ **Complete Activity 2 with the students.**

3. WHY DO WE SIN?

As we've seen in the previous points, sin has its origin in Satan because he's the one who seduces us to disobey the will of God. The method that Satan uses to divert us from God's plans is called "temptation."

○ Ask the students to complete Activity 3.

Satan uses pride, ambition and selfishness of our hearts to tempt us. The essence of all sin is the selfishness that nests in the heart of every human being. In 1 John 2:16, we're warned that temptation can reach us in three ways:

a. The inexhaustible "desires" to satisfy our selfish interests. This is when we make decisions, act and think always putting ourselves first, usurping the place that belongs to God in our lives. This "me first" mentality is known as the "carnal ego" or concupiscence (sinful desire) that's sinful. This is the human will that, instead of submitting to the will of God, lives in rebellion and independence from Him. The person who thinks in this way lives to satisfy the desires of the flesh, that is, his/her physical desires.

b. The "lust of the eyes" refers to the desire to accumulate material goods; things that when we see them, we want to possess them, and wakes up in us greed, envy, and other forms of sin.

c. The "pride of life" refers to the ostentatious, vain way of living and displaying possessions or boasting about what we have.

When Adam and Eve sinned, they led the whole human race to be servants of sin and their own desires, satisfying their whims without regard to God and His purpose for their lives. Consequently, we were contaminated with a force that drags us and predisposes us to evil.

A careful study of the temptation of Adam and Eve, and that of Jesus, will lead us to conclude that temptation always leads us to reject the authority of God and live our life independently of His will.

4. WHY IS SIN SO BAD?

The Bible tells us this truth. With a simple look around us, we can verify how sin is present and destroying the lives of people, families and society. Sin has been and will always be the greatest evil that humans must face.

Sin is one of the big themes of the Bible (God, sin and the Salvation provided by Jesus Christ). Satan tries to deceive us by making us think that sin is of no importance. But the Bible teaches that sin is so large an evil that removing it from the human heart is the only cure. Thus, the one and only Son of God had to die on the cross.

Why did God do this? He did so because the devastating consequences of sin go beyond the individual, extending to society and to the whole of God's creation.

God sent His Son because sin needed a solution, and only God could provide it. Without divine intervention, sin would lead us to self-extermination, and with us, the whole earth.

Let's see what the Bible teaches us about these consequences.

○ Complete Activity 4 with the students.

Sin separates us from God

Because of their sin, Adam and Eve lost the presence of the Holy Spirit who dwelt in them. This left them and all their descendants separated from God. This has been and will continue to be the greatest tragedy in human history, and all the suffering of the inhabitants of the planet started at that point.

Sin separates us from the Creator. Romans 3:23 says: *"For all have sinned and fall short of the glory of God."* Sin separates us from our God because He is holy, and all sin, great or small, is like a dividing wall between us and God.

The greatest pain that a person faces in this life is to live far away from God. Since we were created to be indwelt by the Holy Spirit and to live in harmony with God`s purposes, mankind is now separated from God by sin, and cannot find satisfaction for the deep thirst and spiritual hunger they feel that God alone can fill. This prevents them from being fully happy.

The first couple was the first to go through this devastating experience. They lost their status as children of God. The freedom to serve God was exchanged for the slavery of sin; their joy was changed to shame, their trust turned into fear. Although God loved them, he couldn't ignore the sin that had settled in their lives.

Sin produces guilt

When Adam and Eve sinned, a voice in their conscience made them aware of the error they had made in disobeying God. That's why they felt shame and fear of facing the Creator to assume the consequences of their actions.

Guilt is that feeling that makes us realize that we've done something wrong in the eyes of God, that is, that we've voluntarily transgressed a commandment of God. This guilt is the inner voice that God has put in mankind to remember that sin has consequences. Guilt is associated with the feelings of shame and remorse for what has been done.

Guilt shows us that we are responsible for sins committed. Adam and Eve tried to cast the blame for their sin on someone else, but no other person is responsible for our sin unless they participate with us in a sinful action. In fact, sometimes the Bible condemns entire nations that have sinned against God (Matthew 10:5; Luke 11:29-32).

All people feel guilty for their sin, yet some have developed the capacity to harden their "conscience" and ignore the inner voice that tells them that they are going astray. 2 Corinthians 4:4 teaches us that sin blinds the intellect, and convinces us that it's not important and doesn't lead to major consequences.

However, even though a person's conscience is dormant, before God, he/she remains responsible for their sins. The Bible warns us that the day will come when every person will give an account to God for their actions, and God`s punishment will be in proportion to the guilt.

·································o **Complete Activity 5 with the students.**

The only way to get rid of guilt is by confessing to God the sins one has committed. Adam and Eve confessed their sin, and although they had to face the consequences, they were pardoned. The only way to get rid of guilt is to be forgiven by God.

In the Old Testament, God established the sacrificial system by which people who asked God for forgiveness, were forgiven and freed from guilt. The sin offering was burned, or destroyed, taking the place of the sinner. These sacrifices were the reminder of the Lamb of God who would come to this world, taking upon himself the punishment that our sin deserves. Jesus Christ blotted out our guilt and helped us avoid the death penalty we all deserved. Thankfully Jesus Christ put His life in our place so we don't have to make sacrifices to be forgiven. But we do need to repent and acknowledge our guilt before God.

Sin produces death

Sin as a condition, passed on to us from our first parents, is known as "depravity." Depravity means something that is corrupted or spoiled. This depravity is the opposite of God's holiness. This separation from God, the Giver of Life, if not corrected, leads to eternal separation from the Creator.

In the same way as a man who is dying can be kept alive by machines, the separation of Adam and Eve from God started the spiritual death of the whole human race. So just like the first couple, people today are alive, physically speaking, but are dead because they cannot nourish themselves from the source of Life.

Modern science has proven that even before the moment of birth, our body begins a process of deterioration that finally, years later, ends with physical death. It seems a paradox, but from the time that we're being formed in the womb, our body begins to grow old. Every day after birth, dead cells are released from our body. Some are renewed, some are not, and then even those that are renewed eventually stop and affect our health. The same thing happens with spiritual death. From the day we're born, every human being has a marked destiny - death. Unless we turn to God, this "depravity" will dominate us more and more, manipulating our thinking, hardening our conscience, weakening our reason, leading us to a way of living as slaves of sin and Satan.

This original depravation is present in every person. Every child that's born in this world is born with the inclination to sin in his heart. He's innocent in the sense that he has not committed any sins, but he is not pure.

This state of depravity is not the punishment for the sins of our first parents, but the consequence of sin. Genesis 2:7 says that the penalty for sin set by God is death. This is the payment or retribution that divine justice imposes on the sinner. We must remember that it's God who has designed all the laws that govern the world, both in the natural and in the moral.

⬦ **Complete Activity 6 with the students.**

In the same way, God, who is the only completely righteous being in the universe, has established laws for human beings to live according to them. The disobedience or transgression of these laws deserves the judgment of God, and the penalty that He has established for sin is death.

How can we understand that God can punish someone with such a condemnation? The answer lies in the fact that although God is love, He's also holy and just. If God ceased to be just, he would also cease to be holy. Holiness and divine justice are a serious matter. God cannot coexist or associate with anything unclean or contaminated by sin. The death penalty for the sinner encompasses both physical death and spiritual death. The eternal destiny of one who doesn't live close to God in this life is eternal separation from God and death.

Sin destroys relationship between people

Everyone can see destruction in society. Thousands of years of civilization have helped mankind learn how to destroy more and faster. Human life has lost its value, children are abandoned, people are exploited, sex has become an object of consumption. Crime, violence, and moral depravity have invaded streets, schools, institutions, and the media. The law of the strongest, or the richest, prevails in human dealings and international agreements, while thousands upon thousands upon thousands of people die from war, hunger and disease. The saddest thing is that in most cases, they are deaths that could be avoided with a more "humanitarian" distribution of resources.

Sin spreads death in the world

The destruction of our planet is daily news in the media. Man is turning our world into an arid desert of polluted water and dirty atmosphere, wasting natural resources and killing every living thing that depends on them for their subsistence. This is because sin has an expansive power.

⋯⋯⋯⋯⋯⋯⋯⋯⋯⋯⋯⋯⋯o Complete Activity 7 with the students.

When the first couple sinned, God knew that sin was going to spread to their descendants, and that the solution would not be simple, neither for Him nor for them. His justice was applied to their lives, and they had to face the consequences. But God didn't abandon us in our sins. From there, He began to carry out the plan of our salvation. This plan came to fruition when Jesus Christ died for the sin of all mankind, and when the Holy Spirit could finally come to dwell in the hearts of the children of God.

Definition of key terms

- **Satan:** In Hebrew, it means "adversary." He's also called "the devil," which means slanderer or false accuser. He accuses God by teaching false ideas about Him to the people (Genesis 3:1-7). He also accuses the people before God (Job 1:9, 2:4). Other names he receives are: Apollos (destroyer, Revelation 9:11); Beelzebub (Matthew 12:24); Belial (John 12:31); The god of this age (2 Corinthians 4:4); The prince of this world (John 12:31); The prince of the power of the air (Ephesians 2:2); The ancient serpent (Revelation 20:2); The dragon (Revelation 20:2); The adversary (Matthew 13:39; 1 Peter 5:8); The accuser (Revelation 12:10); The father of lies (John 8:44); Murderer (John 8:44); The evil one (1 John 5:19; Ephesians 6:16) and Morning Star (Isaiah 14:12).

- **Personal Sin:** All those decisions and acts that we voluntarily commit against the will and known purposes of God. Sin carries within itself the desire to rebel against the designs of God, to live according to our own whims (Romans 6:7-11; 7:15; 8:10).

- **Original or acquired sin:** An inherited condition that entered the human race when the first parents sinned against God. This condition predisposes the human being to govern himself and seek his self-satisfaction. It's also known as depravity, innate sin, sinfulness.

- **Physical death:** Occurs at the moment that the organs of our body cease to function and the spirit leaves the body. The physical body, the flesh, the bones, the blood disintegrate, but the spiritual person doesn't die, but continues to exist in a state of waiting until the day of the resurrection of the dead in which each person will be judged by Jesus Christ when we will receive the just reward of God according to how we've lived our life on this earth - in obedience or disobedience to God.

- **Spiritual death:** It's the present state of the person who lives in sin and therefore is separated from God, the source of life. Although the person has physical life, if the Spirit of God doesn't live in him, he's already dead, because his life of sin shows that he rejects the eternal life offered by God through Jesus Christ.

- **Eternal death:** It is intended for those who've rejected the salvation offered through Jesus Christ and persisted during their physical life in their disobedience to God. This spiritual death will occur after the judgment of God, when Satan, the demons and all enemies of God will be punished for their rebellion. It's the opposite of eternal life that the children of God receive.

Summary

Mankind was created to live in relationship with his Creator, but fell into the trap of Satan. Because of his disobedience, he lost the relationship of fellowship with God. The Holy Spirit could not remain dwelling in his life and sin came to settle in the human race with all its terrible consequences.

All of us inherit this depraved condition at birth, predisposing us to sin by withdrawing more and more from the Creator and His purposes for life. This sin rooted in the human heart not only destroys the individual, but also affects his/her relationships and contaminates everything that surrounds him.

But there is hope for humanity, for God has devised a plan to rescue us from sin and to deliver us from its destructive power through His Son Jesus Christ. We can receive full forgiveness of sin by repenting, asking for forgiveness, receiving Jesus as our personal Lord and Savior, and allowing the Holy Spirit of God to restore our lives and guide us to live according to God's purposes.

ACTIVITY 1

Read the following verses and write your own definition of sin. (Romans 6:12; 1 John 3:4; James 4:17)

_____

_____

_____

ACTIVITY 2

What does the Bible teach us about the role of Satan today? With the help of the verses indicated, answer the following questions.

1. What does Satan do to keep people from God? (2 Corinthians 4:4)

_____

2. What does Satan offer to those who consent to serve Him? (Matthew 4:8-10)

_____

3. Who's the one who places limits on the action of Satan in the life of the believer? (Luke 22:313)

_____

4. Who does Satan use to accomplish his purposes? (Ephesians 2:2)

_____

5. What does Satan do with the person after convincing them to sin? (2 Peter 2:19)

_____

ACTIVITY 3

READ THE PASSAGE FROM GENESIS 3:1-6 AND FILL IN THE MISSING WORDS IN THE FOLLOWING SENTENCES ABOUT THE METHODS THAT SATAN USES TO TEMPT HUMAN BEINGS. CHOOSE THE CORRESPONDING WORDS FROM THE FOLLOWING LIST:

DOUBTS, SELFISHNESS, APPETITES, LIAR, INDEPENDENT, WEAKNESSES, LIES.

1. Satan uses the natural and innocent _____ and _____ to accomplish his purposes.

2. Satan injects _____ on God and His Word.

3. Satan _____ about God's good intentions and makes God stand as a _____.

4. Satan wants that the person seeks to be _____ of God.

ACTIVITY 4
Make a list of the immediate consequences of the act of sin that Adam and Eve committed according to Genesis 3:14-24.

_____

_____

_____

ACTIVITY 5
Respond to the following questions based on the Biblical references cited.

1. In Genesis 3:7-13, how did Adam and Eve try to be free from guilt?

_____

2. In Romans 5:1 and 8:1, what's the only way to be free from guilt?

_____

ACTIVITY 6
Mention some natural laws designed by God that provide balance to creation.

_____

_____

ACTIVITY 7
Below is an anecdote by the author, illustrating the expansive power of sin.

Have you happened to be around a wet dog when it starts shaking? In my house, we've had dogs as pets for several years. On one occasion, we had an American Cocker Spaniel female dog, her name was Tracy. As a housewife, I used to bathe her, and since she wasn't very large, we washed her in the laundry sink. It was difficult to reach the towel because she wanted to get out of the pool and shake her wet hair every so often, so in the process she bathed me too. When I finished at last, I had a towel handy and covered her before she began to shake. Can you imagine why? If she got there first, she would splash everything around: walls, washing machine, floor, curtain, window, clean clothes and my face and my hair!

After these enriching experiences with a long-haired dog, we moved on to a boxer. My current dog is called Brownie (yes like the cookies - guess why?). He's very big and we bathe him in the shower. Since he's of a docile race, we're winning the battle. He's very obedient, and when we finish his bath, we close the curtain of the shower and we say to him "Brownie now you shake!" I don't have to clean the entire laundry anymore, just the shower.

But it's quite different when we bathe him in the garden with the hose. There we run first and then we tell him to shake! We're not always able to save ourselves from the spray, so we must shower ourselves afterwards to remove the "dog smell" and to feel human beings again.

Just as dogs cannot avoid shaking out water from their fur, so it's with sin. We cannot prevent our sin from spreading everywhere and permeating everything it touches and everything it does.

Mónica Mastronardi de Fernández

The role of the Holy Spirit in our salvation
Lesson 3

Learning goals:

That the students ...

- Know how the grace of God works through the Holy Spirit to bring us to an encounter with Christ.

- Understand what the Holy Spirit does when he comes to dwell in the life of the new believer.

- Evaluate whether each person in the study has truly experienced the regenerative work of the Holy Spirit in their lives.

Resources

- Have enough plasticine or play dough for each pupil to make a small model of a person.

Introduction

||| Discuss with the class the following problem. |||

Suppose you must go to a place you don't know along a path that you've never traveled where you have to overcome hazards and deviations. Now, you have two options for reaching the destination: a map made by a friend with arrows and signs, or the presence of another friend who knows the way and has offered to accompany and guide you. Which would you choose? What's the safest guide: the map or a person who travels with you?

||| Allow the students to share their opinions. |||

Of course the person, right?

In this lesson, we'll see that this is what the Holy Spirit does. He's the divine person that Jesus Christ has sent us to show us the way to salvation. If we learn to recognize his voice and obey his instructions, we'll arrive safely to heaven.

Bible Study

1. WHO IS THE HOLY SPIRIT?

The Holy Spirit is a person

What does it mean to be a person? When we try to define "person," we obtain answers that relate to our intellectual, emotional and spiritual capacities that have nothing to do with the physical or material part of being human.

For example, in Ephesians 4:30, it states that the Holy Spirit is a person who grieves. The word "grieves" means "to feel sorrow or sadness," and no one can do this unless he or she is a person.

In Acts 13:2, we see that the Holy Spirit spoke to the believers of the church in Antioch, telling them to send Paul and Barnabas as missionaries to evangelize in other cities. The Holy Spirit is a divine person, who has the ability to dwell in our lives and communicate with our spirit, guiding us to live in holiness.

||| Read together Romans 8:14: *"For those who are led by the Spirit of God are the children of God."* |||

The Spirit is omnipotent and sovereign

............................o **Ask the students to complete Activity 1.**

The Holy Spirit is God, as well as the Father, and Jesus Christ, the Son. As God, He has all the power and authority to act in our lives and intervene in human affairs. Today, He acts through guiding the people of God so that the gospel of Christ can extend geographically, and more people can come to know the Lord as Savior and serve Him with their lives.

The Spirit has power and sovereignty to act where there are children of God who are willing to let themselves be used by Him. Despite being a powerful and sovereign God, He respects our free will and will only act in our lives when he finds a willingness to cooperate with Him.

2. WHAT DOES THE HOLY SPIRIT DO FOR OUR SALVATION?

Keeps us and gives us life

When Adam and Eve sinned, God set in motion a plan to save mankind and bring them back to His love and to live in His will. This love of God that seeks to attract us is known as "grace."

This grace of God is what allows human beings to continue to live, even though they are spiritually dead in their sins, and have the opportunity to know and accept the way of Salvation that Christ provides for them. The grace of God is what allows life to continue in this world, and for us all to keep breathing.

The grace of God is what enables men and women to retain some of the capacities with which they were created in the image of God, such as wisdom, the capacity to feel mercy, to show solidarity, to love, to invent valuable things, to write good laws, honor, friendship, humor, artistic ability, seeking God in moments of need or wanting to know where his life comes from and what the purpose of existence is.

Grace is administered by the Holy Spirit and is what has stopped mankind from turning to evil. The Holy Spirit works many everyday miracles that are often imperceptible to us: He causes rain to fall, makes life begin in the womb, allows us to heal when we breathe, gives rest to our body and mind when we sleep, helps us to have creative ideas, allows us to learn, grow, mature, allows us to fall in love and much more.

He leads us to Jesus Christ

In the parable of the prodigal son (Luke 15:20), the father, who represents God the Father, takes the initiative to actively wait for his son. Time and again the Word speaks to us about God loving us and desiring us to return to fellowship with Him, even when we lived in sin. As I John 4:10, 19 says, *"This is love: not that we loved God, but that he loved us and sent his Son as an atoning sacrifice for our sins…We love because he first loved us."* This grace of God who seeks us and draws us to Himself is known as "prevenient grace."

It is the Holy Spirit who prepares us for an encounter with God. He helps us to understand, to desire and to respond to this grace that offers us a new life in Christ.

Ask the students to observe the graphic in Activity 2.

In Activity 2, we can see that there are at least four factors through which the prevenient grace of God works to help people recognize that they need Jesus in their lives: 1) the inner action of the Holy Spirit convincing of sin; 2) the prayers of the people of God in favor of that person, 3) the Word of God (through testimony, preaching, reading, teaching or other means) and 4) the receptivity of the person to the grace of God.

He produces sorrow for sins committed, and faith in Christ for salvation

Ask a student to read John 16:8-11.

Here the role of the Holy Spirit in the life of the sinner is described, opening our understanding and helping us recognize our condition as separated from God and without hope. Without this action of the Holy Spirit in our hearts, none of us would realize that the sinful facts of our life have separated us from our Creator.

It is the Holy Spirit who makes us feel guilt and sorrow for the sins we have committed, makes our conscience uneasy, moves us in our feelings and guides our will towards God. If we cooperate with the grace of God, we'll attain salvation. However, the Word also warns us that we can resist grace.

Complete Activity 3.

Without the action of the Holy Spirit and God's prevenient grace, there would be no hope of salvation for us. That is why the apostle Paul exclaimed in Ephesians 2:8, *"For it's by grace you have been saved, through faith—and this is not from yourselves, it's the gift of God."* Or as expressed in the Message, a modern day version: *"It's God's gift from start to finish! We don't play the major role. If we did, we'd probably go around bragging that we'd done the whole thing!"*

The Spirit comes to live in us when we accept Christ as Savior

From Old Testament times, the prophets had announced that the Holy Spirit would come to live in our hearts (Isaiah 59:21, Ezekiel 37:14, 39:29, Joel 2:28, 29).

Ask a student to read Ephesians 1:13.

Paul says that when we believe in Jesus as Savior, *"we were sealed with the Holy Spirit."* This means that once the sins committed have been cleansed from our lives, God gives us the Holy Spirit to live in us, and this is the "sign" or the seal indicating that we are now sons and daughters of God.

In ancient times, the seal (usually the ring) was like the signature of a person and declared ownership over wherever the mark had been stamped. It also indicated authenticity. It's similar in our day to authenticating the signature in a work of art by experts, which assigns true value to the work. Or when the public notary (clerk or lawyer) authenticates a signature with his seal indicating its veracity as "This signature or document is valid."

This is what God does when he gives us His Spirit. He points to us as "his own" and no longer belonging to sin. From there, the Spirit begins to guide us in a series of changes or transformations throughout our lives to help us become more and more like Jesus.

In Acts 19:1-7, we see the experience of a group of new Christians to whom the apostle Paul asks them a question: *"Did you receive the Holy Spirit when you believed? They answered, "No, we haven't even heard that there is a Holy Spirit."*

It is important for us Christians to be aware of the presence of the Holy Spirit in our lives, for this is indispensable for continual growth in our experience of salvation, staying near Christ and far from sin. The Holy Spirit is present in our lives so that we can relate to Him and allow Him to speak and guide us in every aspect of our life.

The Holy Spirit imparts a new Life.

||| Ask a student to read 1 Corinthians 15:22. |||

Here the apostle Paul divides mankind into two large groups: those who belong to the generation of Adam and those who are with Christ. There is a big difference between these two groups, some are walking towards death and others are identified because they have been given new life.

Once, a man named Nicodemus came to see Jesus. This man was on a spiritual quest and asked Jesus how he could have eternal life with God. Jesus taught him that the only way is to be born again (John 3:3). He then goes on to explain that this is not a physical but a spiritual birth, and can only be brought about within the human heart by the Spirit of God. This spiritual rebirth is from the inside out. It's a change that takes place inside, but whose evidence is perceived on the outside.

||| Ask a student to read Romans 8:2 and ask the class:
What is the name of the Holy Spirit here? |||

He's called the "Spirit of life" and we are told that the Spirit frees us from "the law of sin and death".

||| Ask the students: What word does Paul use in 2 Corinthians 3:6 and 5:17 to teach
about the work of the Spirit in the human heart? |||

How is the Spirit described in 2 Corinthians 3:6? He is called the "giver of life" which implies regeneration. Regeneration is correcting something or someone who has degenerated, restoring them in their proper function and even improving it. In 2 Corinthians 5:17 it says, *"Therefore, if anyone is in Christ, the new creation has come: The old has gone, the new is here!"*

||| Distribute the pieces of plasticine or play dough to students and have them make a
model of a human figure. |||

Then move among your students and disfigure some of the models they made (pricking them or scrunching them in your hands), while explaining to them that what you are doing is the same thing that sin has done in us, making us lose our beauty, our purity. In other words, the image of God is blurred. Now ask them to do with those models what God has done in their lives, in other words to repair the damage, to return their identity to their work of art.

Watch the students who had to do the whole process again and then ask why they made the model again instead of repairing it? Let them express their ideas about it by relating what they have done to the meaning of "regenerating."

▌▌▌ One of the greatest prophecies regarding our salvation is found in Ezekiel 36:26-27. Ask a student to read those verses. ▌▌▌

Jesus came that we might have life. This means that the believer receives spiritual life at the moment of salvation. The Bible says that when we repent of our sins and place our faith in Christ as our Lord and Savior, we are made "children of God" at that very moment (John 1:12).

The first thing the Spirit of God does is to *"remove your heart of stone and give you a heart of flesh."* In other words, the Holy Spirit gives us a new heart. This new heart, unlike the other one which was rebellious and disobedient, is sensitive to the voice of God. This is what the Bible calls "conversion," a radical turnabout, a "U" turn, or a new beginning. This is a miracle, a "spiritual heart surgery." All of us need to change our self-centered way of living to live a life of obedience to God.

········o **Instruct the students to look at the charts in Activity 4 where you can see how the heart of the person who is born again changes.**

All this work is made possible by the perfect sacrifice of Jesus on the cross of Calvary. He paid with his blood the price of our salvation by putting his life in our place and receiving the punishment that we deserved for our sin. Jesus Christ rescued us from a life of spiritual death where we were slaves to sin, he cleanses us from all our sin, and he has sent His Spirit to dwell in our being.

The Bible says that this Christian is a spiritual baby (1 Peter 2:2) who needs to grow and strengthen in the Word, in service and in obedience to God in all areas of his life.

The process of sanctification begins at salvation

The only way to live in holiness is to allow the Holy Spirit to dwell in us. "Our spirit was created to be indwelt by the Holy Spirit who imparts holiness of character." This intimate presence of God was lost when Adam and Eve fell into sin. That is why throughout human history, God has called men and women to be holy, as He is Holy. Once the Holy Spirit dwells in the human heart, the physical body becomes the temple or dwelling place of the Holy Spirit (1 Corinthians 3:16). From then on, the Spirit that dwells in us will try to keep us from sin and close to Jesus.

That is why in the New Testament Christians are called saints. A saint is a person who has been born again and now belongs to the family of God.

▌▌▌ Ask the students: What then does the Spirit of God do in our hearts, according to Jeremiah 31:33? ▌▌▌

Once the Spirit has created a receptive attitude in our hearts, he writes within the human being the law of God and enables us to live accordingly.

The experience of being "born again" is also known as "initial sanctification." This is the beginning

---

[1] Wesley L. Duewel in *"God offers you his great Salvation"*. Nappanee, Indiana: Evangel Publishing House, 2000, p. 21.

of a life tuned to the will of God. It means that we are no longer under the rule of sin, but under the Lordship of Jesus. Therefore, our lives are gradually being changed according to God's purpose. The Spirit of Jesus impels us to do good and reject evil. Paul is speaking of this power when he tells us in Romans 6:14, "For sin shall no longer be your master, because you are not under the law, but under grace." Sin has no power over the children of God.

We become members of the people of God

][[[Ask a student to read Galatians 4:4-7.]]][

Adoption is a wonderful act of God's grace through which God declares us "His children." This can happen because we have been forgiven, justified and regenerated by God. Forgiveness and justification take care of the problem of the blame and pain that sin causes us.

Regeneration and adoption provide us with a new identity as members of the family of God, with rights and a special heritage

○ Ask the class to complete Activity 5.

[[[Ask another student to read 1 Peter 2:9-10.]]]

The apostle Peter says clearly: *"Once you were not a people, but now you are the people of God ..."* The emphasis of this verse is that we now belong to a different people, with characteristics, laws and purpose different from the other peoples of the earth. This nation is not limited to a national race or flag, but extends beyond political, racial, cultural or geographical boundaries and embraces the entire universal family of God.

This people is called by their Lord to consecrate themselves or to sanctify themselves, that is, to give themselves completely to the mission entrusted to them by God, to proclaim the good news of the Lord and to make disciples of Christ throughout the world (Matthew 28: 19-20).

Definition of key terms

- **Grace:** the free love of God towards the human race (Ephesians 2:4-10).
- **Repentance:** Necessary experience to receive the work of salvation in Christ. It consists of feeling deep sorrow for having sinned against God and the desire to turn away from the practice of sin to live in obedience to God.
- **Initial Sanctification:** It begins with the experience of the new birth when the Holy Spirit comes to dwell in the newly converted believer. This is where the process of growth or maturity of the Christian begins, following the example of Jesus, and living closer to God.

Summary

The Lord, by the power of His Spirit, draws us to salvation. For this, the Spirit makes us feel sorrow and guilt for sin in order to lead us to repentance, to ask for forgiveness and for Jesus to be the Savior and Lord of our lives.

When God forgives us and cleanses us of our sin, He puts His Spirit in us and declares us to be just or holy before Him. The experience of salvation is a rebirth from the inside out, that is, our hearts are transformed by the Spirit. God adopts us into his family and we're united to his people. Our life becomes the temple and dwelling place of the Holy Spirit, who imparts to us the life of Christ, guides us in continuous growth, and shows us how to live in holiness and strength to follow the model Jesus gave us.

Activity Worksheet

ACTIVITY 1
Read Acts 8:39-40 and answer the following questions:

1. What name does the Holy Spirit receive in this passage?

_____

2. How does this name relate to the promise Jesus made to his disciples in John 14:16-18?

_____

3. Where did the Spirit lead Philip and for what purpose?

_____

ACTIVITY 2
Graphic: The four forces that operate to bring the sinful person to Christ.

Prevenient Grace

Prayers
of the People
of God
Jn. 17:29
Prov. 15:29

Receptivity
to
Grace
Mt. 13:14-15

Holy Spirit
Rom. 2:4, John. 16:8

Word of God
Acts 26:18

MAN   WOMAN

Description in Romans 8:7-8

ACTIVITY 3
Summarize the teaching of each of these verses with regard to how human beings can resist the grace of God that works in their life to lead them to salvation.

• Ephesians 4:30, Acts 5:9, Hebrews 10:19, Isaiah 63:10

_____

_____

_____

ACTIVITY 4
Graphic: Comparison between a life in sin and born-again Christian

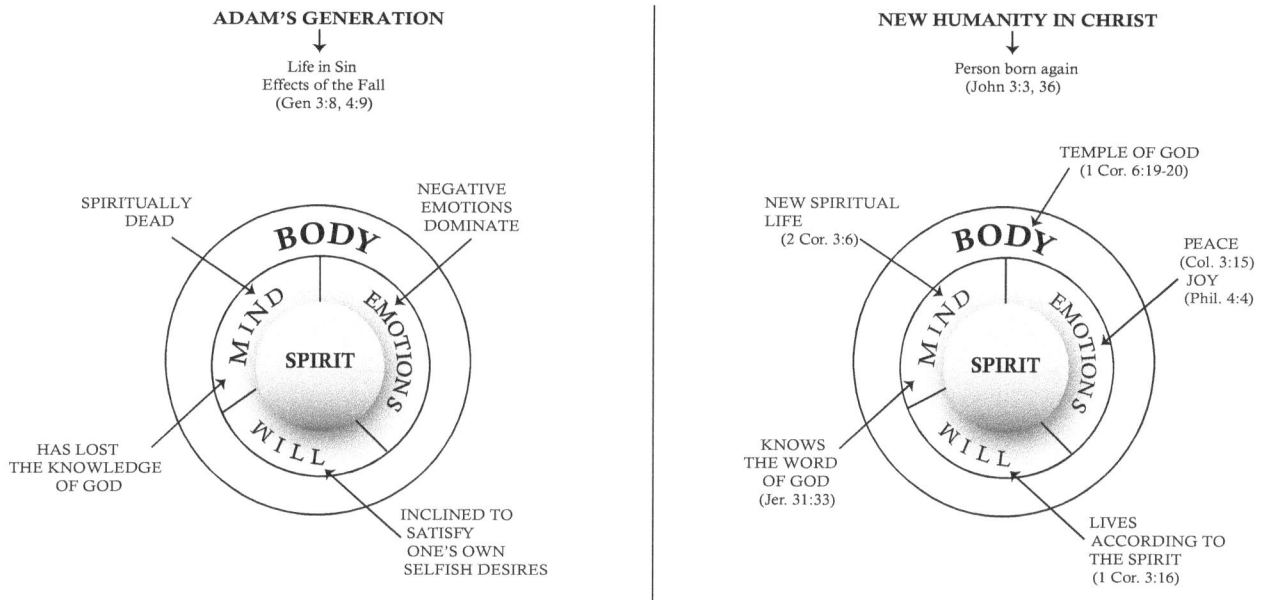

ADAM'S GENERATION
↓
Life in Sin
Effects of the Fall
(Gen 3:8, 4:9)

SPIRITUALLY DEAD

NEGATIVE EMOTIONS DOMINATE

BODY
MIND — EMOTIONS
SPIRIT
WILL

HAS LOST THE KNOWLEDGE OF GOD

INCLINED TO SATISFY ONE'S OWN SELFISH DESIRES

NEW HUMANITY IN CHRIST
↓
Person born again
(John 3:3, 36)

TEMPLE OF GOD
(1 Cor. 6:19-20)

NEW SPIRITUAL LIFE
(2 Cor. 3:6)

PEACE
(Col. 3:15)
JOY
(Phil. 4:4)

BODY
MIND — EMOTIONS
SPIRIT
WILL

KNOWS THE WORD OF GOD
(Jer. 31:33)

LIVES ACCORDING TO THE SPIRIT
(1 Cor. 3:16)

ACTIVITY 5
Below is an explanation of each of the terms that describe what God does so that we can be cleansed from sin. The words will be divided among the students so that, individually or in groups, a definition of the terms can be written in simple vocabulary, using illustrations to better understand the meaning (as for a 5 year old). Definitions will then be shared with the rest of the class.

- **Propitiation:** To propitiate, to make possible something that was impossible. It is the reconciling action between man and God, effected by Jesus Christ on the cross. Through the generous surrender of Christ in giving his life for us, and taking on himself the punishment we deserve, God forgives us, making possible the reconciliation of every sinner with his Creator (John 3:16).

- **Conviction of sin:** It is the result of the action of the Holy Spirit in the heart of a person, making them feel guilty and seeking forgiveness so that the relationship can be restored (John 16: 8).

- **Conversion:** It is the act of believing in the Lord Jesus Christ and sincerely repenting. It's evident in a change of attitude of the person who decides to take a new direction in his/her life in obedience to God. In the act of conversion, God forgives the sins we've committed. This is made possible thanks to the death of Jesus Christ on the cross for us. The repentant person receives a new spiritual life, and can grow in knowledge and service to God (Romans 6:4, 12:2, 2 Corinthians 5:17, Ephesians 4:22-24).

- **Justification:** It is the term used by the apostle Paul to express the divine grace that forgives the repentant sinner and makes him "innocent" before God, declaring him free from guilt and worthy of fellowship with his Creator (Romans 4:25, 5:18).

- **Regeneration:** It is the restoration work performed by the Spirit of God in the person who accepts Christ as his personal Savior. Regeneration means to start out anew, to be born again

(John 3:3).

- **Reconciliation:** Describes the restoration of broken relationships between humans and God as a result of sin. The initiative for reconciliation was the initiative of God and was carried out when He sent His Son as intermediary. God's children now have a responsibility to continue this ministry of reconciliation so that many people will have the opportunity to enjoy a harmonious relationship with the Creator. It is in this sense that Christians are "ambassadors", sent by God as their emissaries to every man, woman and child to bring them to the reunion with Him (Romans 5:10; Matthew 5:24:2 Corinthians 5:18).

- **Adoption:** It is the act of love by which God adopts the new believer as his son or daughter and makes him/her "co-heir with Christ" of the blessings God has prepared for his children (John 1:12, Romans 8:16).

_____

_____

_____

_____

_____

_____

PRAYER

Thank God for the benefits He has given you by adopting you into His Family.

1. God has made me his child: John 1:1-12, Romans 8:14-16

2. I am Christ's brother: Matthew 12:46-50

3. The Spirit gives me a new family relationship: Romans 8:14-16

4. He has given me new relationships in the family of God: 1 Corinthians 12

5. He has given me unrestricted entrance into the presence of God: Hebrews 10:19-20

6. I will have an eternal inheritance: Romans 8:17-25

My Notes

The human part of Salvation
Lesson 4

Learning goals:

That the students ...

- Understand the human response God requires to give us salvation.
- Recognize what constitutes the faith that pleases God, not intellectual knowledge, or temporal faith, but faith that trusts fully in Jesus.
- Assess how deeply their commitment to following Jesus as a disciple has been to this day.
- Have the opportunity to repent if needed.

Resources

- A key chain with various keys.
- An empty chair.

Introduction

We live in a time when people expect God to solve all their problems. As a consequence, we tend to blame God for everything that happens on the planet and in our lives.

In the previous lesson, we saw that the whole initiative of salvation comes from the Creator. However, we also know that God doesn't impose his salvation by force on anyone. It's for this reason that we can speak of the human part in salvation. In this sense, in order for God to perform his complete work of salvation, he needs our cooperation. Without our acceptance of His conditions and our sincere willingness to straighten out our whole life according to His Word, salvation can not come to fruition. What we mean is that this is a work with two parts that mutually cooperate with each other.

In this lesson, we'll study how our actions and decisions allow Jesus' work of salvation to be effective in the life of every person who seeks it.

Bible Study

1. RECOGNIZE THE PERSONAL NEED TO BE SAVED

It's of the utmost importance that we recognize the need to be saved, for in Romans 3:23, the apostle Paul declares, "*... for all have sinned and fall short of the glory of God.*" To fall short means that if we don't accept the salvation offered by God through Jesus Christ, our eternal destiny will lead to death and eternal punishment.

||| Ask a student to read Isaiah 53:6. |||

The Bible reveals that we were not made for death, but to live in eternal fellowship with our Creator. Sadly, sin made a wall of separation between man and God. Only through the work of Jesus on the cross can we return to the original plan.

The Holy Spirit tries by many ways to "convince" us of our state. He brings conviction to our lives so that we recognize that we have a problem with sin and that the only way out of this problem is to turn to God. There are two ways to respond to this revelation of the Holy Spirit: with humility, accepting our need and impotence to rid ourselves of evil or pride, or refusing to repent. In the Bible, we find several examples of people who, having confessed their sin, hardened their hearts and therefore couldn't be forgiven.

Guide the class in completing Activity 1.

We live in a world where there is little preaching about sin. Some preachers prefer to talk about God's love, prosperity, healing, miracles, i.e., only the things we might "get" from God. Because of this, many people go through life ignoring their big problem called SIN. However, conviction of sin isn't enough either. It doesn't help us to wake people from their spiritual numbness to convince them of the evil in which they are submerged if we do nothing to help them out of this problem.

God doesn't abandon us when we're burdened with guilt. He leads us to radical change. God's call to repentance is a proclamation of hope.

2. WHAT IS REPENTANCE?

The word "repent" that's used in the biblical text is the Greek term 'metanoia' that means "change of mind and life." This word infers the idea of change of route, a 180 degree turn heading in the opposite direction. The way of God is opposed to the path of sinful man and the path of the Devil.

Repentance is a complete change in the way we feel, think and live.

[[[Ask a student to read 2 Corinthians 7:6-11.]]]

Have sorrow for your sin

Paul had learned about the sinful life of some people in the church and wrote them a letter to help them understand the sinful condition they were in. By means of Titus, he received the news that these brothers had recognized their need and were saddened. But this was a "good" sorrow because it had led them to repent of their sins.

This sadness isn't a mere pain or remorse, but led to a change in their attitudes. Sorrow for sin is the physical or emotional manifestation of intellectual conviction. Sometimes the person breaks into tears like Simon Peter when he denied Jesus. The Scripture tells us that he "wept bitterly."

In verse 10, *"Godly sorrow brings repentance that leads to salvation and leaves no regret, but worldly sorrow brings death,"* Paul points out the difference between this sadness and common sadness. The sadness that the world produces doesn't lead to good outcomes. When Judas betrayed Jesus, he was sad but he took his own life. The sadness of the world is often a selfish sadness. The human being mourns in his sinful condition but feels sorry for himself. Instead, the sadness that God "works" in us produces humiliation, that is, a broken heart that is poured out before the Lord God asking for His help.

Confess your Sins

Proverbs 28:13 tells us that *"Whoever conceals their sins doesn't prosper, but the one who confesses and renounces them finds mercy."* Confession is the recognition of personal guilt for the sin committed, that is, to be accountable to God for all the evil one has done (bad thoughts, bad deeds and bad words) and asking for forgiveness.

[[[Ask a student to read Psalms 32:5.]]]

In this Psalm, David praises God for having forgiven him of his sin, and he expresses two very important truths:

1. We need to recognize that our guilt and sin are ours alone. It's a personal matter. David assumes absolute responsibility for his sin before God. Although our sin hurts other people, every sin is an offense to God. David said: *"Against you only, have I sinned and done what is evil in your sight..."* (Psalm 51:4)

2. Declare your inability and impotence to rid yourself of the burden of your sin. Sin committed is a debt against God. No human being can "pay off" this debt of sin on their own, trying to erase this offense to God's holiness. Only by trusting in Christ as the only and sufficient Savior can we be forgiven (1 Corinthians 2:39).

It's also sometimes necessary to confess sin to people who we may have offended, and make restitution as far as possible. The Holy Spirit is responsible for bringing to our memory the offenses (sins) done to people or groups of people who have been harmed by our sin. We need to confess and ask for their forgiveness.

Decide to abandon sinning

True repentance leads to renunciation of sin.

▌▌▌ Ask a volunteer to read Isaiah 55:7. ▌▌▌

Just as human feelings respond to the conviction of sin and the sadness produced by God to lead us to repentance, the confession of sin, the renunciation of sin, and the acts of restitution are carried out by our wills. God in his grace places in our heart a feeling of disgust toward all kinds of sin. But we still need to exercise our will to say 'no' whenever the opportunity for sin looms near.

The passage quoted in Proverbs 28:13 above tells us that whoever confesses their sin and *"renounces it shall receive mercy."* This doesn't mean that we can somehow earn our salvation, but our positive response to God is indispensable if this work of cleansing is to be completed in us. That's why 1 John 1:9 says: *"If we confess our sins, he is faithful and just and will forgive us our sins and purify us from all unrighteousness."*

3. PUT ALL YOUR FAITH IN CHRIST

▌▌▌ Read Ephesians: "For it's by grace you have been saved, through faith—and this isn't from yourselves, it's the gift of God..." ▌▌▌

Again, we see how this verse points us to the two people who participate in salvation. The part of God - grace, the human part - faith. The salvation that God offers us is conditioned by our faith. At the same time, Paul makes it clear that the source of salvation is God and not human beings, since even this ability to believe is a gift from God. The Holy Spirit is the one who works in our lives so that we turn to God through the gift of faith. Faith is what enables us to fully trust Jesus Christ for our salvation.

What's this faith that God expects of us so that He can save us? There are various types of faith.

▌▌▌ Show the keyring with the keys and say something like this while looking at the keys: Here I have the keys that I use frequently. This is the key of the car, this is the key to my office, that of the church, that of my house. All are quite similar to each other, are made of metal, look quite similar, but only one - the correct one - is the one that opens the door of my house. I can try to open the door of my house with any key, but only if I use the correct one will it open. The same thing happens with faith. There are several types of faith, but only one is the faith that opens the door to salvation. ▌▌▌

Let's look at these types of faith. The faith of some people is a historical faith. They believe in Jesus as they believe in ... (say the name of an important person in the history of their country). This faith is intellectual or cognitive. We believe that this person existed or exists, but we don't really know him.

The faith of other people resembles a camping ice chest. We have it stored in the garage or in the cellar of the house, it's accumulating dust and we don't remember it until we use it once or maybe twice a year. If we have lent it to someone and they didn't return it, then - when we need it - we remember that we must reclaim it. Some people have a "temporary" faith, a faith that makes its appearance when we are in need. We remember God and cry out to Him to ask for work, to ask for health, to ask Him to protect us on a trip. It's a faith that we use only at some points in our lives.

But **saving faith** is very different from intellectual faith and temporal faith.

▌▌▌ Now bring the empty chair to you and stand next to it. As you speak, look at the chair and make suitable adaptations with your arms and face that reinforce the meaning of the words. ▌▌▌

Let's use this chair to understand saving faith. Look at this chair, it looks strong and I think if I sit on it, I won't fall. What do you think? Will it hold my weight? I can stare at the chair, saying things about its construction or appearance, but never sitting on it. On the contrary, saving faith is that faith in which I make the decision to put all my trust in the chair and I sit in it, or I deposit my (...) kilograms (or pounds) trusting that it's going to support me and will not let me fall to the ground.

Such is saving faith. Only if we place all our trust in Jesus Christ can we be saved! Your faith may be weak, it may be dubious, but the important thing isn't the quality of your faith, but in whom you put your faith.

▌▌▌ Ask a student to read John 3:16-17. ▌▌▌

John tells us that the Son didn't come into the world to condemn the world, but *"that the world through him might be saved."* There is no other way of salvation. Putting our faith in the right person is fundamental if we want to be saved. It's okay to admire good people who are living or dead, but these people cannot do anything to cleanse our sin. Only the blood of Jesus Christ shed on the cross has the power to forgive us of all evil (1 John 1:7-9).

Ask the students to complete Activity 2.

4. RECEIVE JESUS AS SAVIOUR AND LORD

In John 13:13, Jesus said, *"You call me 'Teacher' and 'Lord,' and rightly so, for that is what I am."* Jesus attributes two titles or functions in this verse, as" Teacher" and "Lord ". What did the people of that time understand when they heard Jesus use these titles about himself?

First, let's look at "Teacher" which comes from the Greek "epistates" and means one who teaches and cares for his students or disciples. In those days, there were many teachers who taught the Word of God, but the style of Jesus was different from theirs because his teaching went beyond giving lessons. He taught by example, showing them how they should live.

The word "Lord" or "kurios" in Greek means "one who dominates and directs everything that is his and implies subjection and obedience of the people who belong to him."

Lord is a word that in those days was used only for God in the case of the Jews, and only for the emperor "Cesar" in the case of the Romans. The belief of those times was that the emperor was a god and that when he died, he became part of the great number of Roman gods. There was even the death penalty for those who called someone other than the emperor 'Lord', and some Christians were sentenced to death because of this.

The title of Lord for Jesus tells us that He is in control when He saves us and we become His followers. We are a precious possession for Him. The kind of dominion that Christ exercises over us isn't like a tyrant or a king who uses people for self-indulgence. The kind of leadership the Bible is talking about is service.

As we've seen, asking for forgiveness for our sins involves making the decision to change our lives. This change is from controlling our lives ourselves to becoming followers of the Lord Jesus Christ.

Ask the class to complete Activity 3 to see why the new believer needs to be subject to the lordship of Christ.

5. BELIEVE THAT YOU HAVE BEEN BORN AGAIN

Ask a volunteer to read John 6:47.

All who have been forgiven of their sins have been reborn to a new life. Before that, they were alive physically, but spiritually dead because they had no eternal life. But since the Holy Spirit came to live in their being, they have spiritual LIFE. This life extends beyond physical death. It's an eternal life, which will not end but will allow us to be with Jesus Christ and serve Him forever. However, this truth is of no use if we don't believe it and don't live according to it.

Also, the apostle Paul says in 2 Corinthians 5:17 that if we are in Christ *"we're a new creation."* This new creature comes to replace the person I used to be. That old creature that lived in sin must cease to exist to give space for this new person we're going to grow into. Christian baptism rightly represents this spiritual truth. It symbolizes that the person has died to sin (when immersed in the water) and has been reborn to a new life as a disciple of Christ.

If we believe with our whole heart that we've been made new creatures, this inner conviction will help us to look at ourselves and the circumstances that surround us differently. We no longer have to continue to sin. Now we are sons and daughters of God, created to live in holiness and serve the purposes of God in this world.

Believing that we have been made new is indispensable because it's the starting point for a healthy development in this new life, allowing the life of Jesus to grow within us and expand to fill our whole being.

....o **Guide the students to complete Activity 4.**

6. COMMITMENT TO PERSEVERE IN DISCIPLESHIP

Every Christian is called to be a disciple of Jesus. This implies accepting Jesus as the Teacher who will show us how to live to please God in everything we think, say and do. The Christian never ceases to be a disciple, because learning to be saints like Jesus is something that will take us a lifetime.

Every Christian must make this decision to be an apprentice. This requires humiliation and recognizing that everything we have learned in our lives has no value if compared to the wealth of wisdom that Christ wants to give us.

At the same time, discipleship isn't only intellectual knowledge, nor only learning to keep spiritual truths in our minds, but to treasure them in our hearts and allow these truths to gradually transform all that we are and what we do. The apostle Paul counsels his spiritual son Timothy in 1 Timothy 4:16 to care for his way of life as he cares for the doctrine that he learns and teaches. In the next lesson, we'll talk more about how a person who is born again ought to live.

....o **Complete Activity 5.**

Finish with a few moments of prayer for the personal needs that arise from the previous activity.

Definition of key terms

- **Faith:** This word is used in three ways: to believe in something you cannot feel or see; the action of putting all confidence in Christ for salvation; or it can also point to the core beliefs of Christianity.

- **Gift:** Abilities received from God through the Holy Spirit to perform some Christian service. For example; Teaching, providing for the needs of others, healing the sick, among others.

- **Repentance:** A necessary experience to be saved by Christ. It consists in feeling deep pain for having sinned against God and wanting to turn away from the practice of sin to live a holy life.

- **Discipleship:** The life-long learning process through which we grow more and more like Jesus. Discipleship begins with conversion and continues to the end of life.

Summary

Salvation in Christ isn't something that happens accidentally: it's a plan designed by the eternal God. At the same time, this plan isn't imposed on the human being. That's why salvation involves a personal recognition of the need to be saved.

Salvation cannot come without genuine repentance on the part of the sinful person, which leads him to humble himself and ask God's forgiveness for his sins.

Salvation requires an act of faith on the part of the repentant sinner and an absolute surrender to Jesus Christ by accepting Him as the only Savior and Lord of life.

This experience will remain fresh in us as long as we commit ourselves to being disciples of the Master all our lives.

Activity Worksheet

ACTIVITY 1
Investigate in the Bible some examples of people who acknowledged their sin but hardened their hearts.

Text	Who is it about?	What was the sin that was confessed?	How did their life end?
Exodus 9:27,34			
Numbers 22:34; 23:10 y 31:8			
Joshua 7:20			
1 Samuel 15:24			
Matthew 27:4			

ACTIVITY 2
Complete the following list of characteristics of saving faith by looking at the Bible verses and completing the missing words in the sentences.

a. Submit the _____ to God (Psalm 37:5).

b. Believing in _____ (John 3:15).

c. Become _____ in the heart (Romans 6:17).

d. _____ with the heart (Romans 10:9-10).

e. Believing the Bible to be _____ (2 Timothy 3:16-17).

f. Put all your _____ in God (Hebrews 2:13).

g. Invite _____ into your life (Revelation 3:20).

ACTIVITY 3.
Answer the following questions in teams of two or three students.

a. Share testimonies of some difficulties you've experienced in your lives and how the Lord has helped.

b. Compare your testimonies with the difficulties mentioned in the following verses: John 16:33, 1 Corinthians 10:13, Ephesians 6:10-12

c. According to Matthew 6:24 and Romans 6:16, what is the reason why Christ must have dominion in your life?

d. What important decision does Paul beg us to make in Romans 12:1?

e. What practical implications would this decision bring to our life?

Activity Worksheet - Lesson 4

ACTIVITY 4.
Read Romans 8:15-17 and respond.

a) Are Christians different than other people?

_____

_____

b) In what sense?

_____

_____

c) What do they have that makes them different?

_____

_____

ACTIVITY 5.
Have I really had this experience of being saved? Answer the following questions with yes or no.

a. Have you felt sorrow for your sins?   _____

b. Did that sorrow lead you to repent sincerely before God?   _____

c. Have you asked God's forgiveness for your sins?   _____

d. Have you again committed the same sins for which you repented?   _____

3. Have you trusted in Jesus, and only in Him, as Savior for you?   _____

f. Can you say that at this moment, Jesus is the Lord of your whole life?   _____

g. Do you have a deep commitment as a follower of Jesus?   _____

h. Do you think others think you are a faithful disciple of Jesus?   _____

i. Are you sure that you're now a son/daughter of God?   _____

j. If not, would you like to have that security in your life today?   _____

Tell the teacher what areas of your life you have answered no. If in truth and with all your heart you want to repent of your sins and to be saved, don't leave it for another week. Ask the Lord according to your need and fully trust that He will do His part and make you a new creature.

RECOMMENDED READINGS
- Isaiah 57
- Isaiah 61
- Psalm 51
- Psalm 134
- Psalm 147

Salvation: an experience that transforms
Lesson 5

Learning goals:

That the students ...

- Know the internal changes that are reflected in the lifestyle of a new disciple
- Share their testimonies about the evidence of the new birth in their lives.
- Be sure that they're allowing the Holy Spirit to guide and reorder their lives according to the teachings of Jesus.

Resources

- Blackboard and chalk or white board and markers

Introduction

In previous lessons, we studied the part of God and the human part in the experience of salvation. The miracle of the new birth marks the beginning of a series of internal changes and external transformations that the Holy Spirit directs in our lives.

In this lesson, we'll talk about these external and internal evidences of salvation that show that the Holy Spirit has come to dwell in our hearts and has begun the transformation of the way we think and live. Internal changes can only be appreciated by the same person, but the process of external transformation in how they live their way of life can be appreciated by everyone around them. This evidence of change in thinking, speaking, and behaving is overwhelming evidence that repentance has been sincere and that the person has indeed been born again.

John the Baptist was the one who came before Jesus announcing to the people of his time that they should repent of their sins. John baptized in water those who confessed with their mouth their repentance. Nevertheless, John doubted the sincerity of some people because they had a double life. On the one hand, they were religiously fulfilling all that the Jewish law pointed out, but on the other, their life was full of sin. That's why John told them to go and *"Produce fruit in keeping with repentance"* (Matthew 3:8).

We will speak of these fruits in this lesson, and to do this, we'll answer the question: what are the internal and external changes in the person's life that show that he has been born again?

Bible Study

1. A HEART FULL OF HAPPINESS

The story of King David always moves us.

The Bible shows David as he was with his weaknesses, but also with a tremendous sensitivity to let himself be guided by the Lord. He was a poet and wrote many songs found in the book of Psalms. Psalm 32 is one where David describes the joy of having been forgiven after the chain of sins committed in connection with his adultery with Bathsheba.

||| Ask a student to read Psalm 32. |||

David tries to express in words the great change that has taken place inside him when he was forgiven. All the negative feelings that sin had caused in his life had disappeared and had been replaced by feeling blessed.

This word "blessed" implies happiness. This isn't any kind of temporary happiness like when we receive good news, but a more permanent deep joy that comes to the heart of the new Christian. This happiness is possible because now God, the only source of true happiness, dwells in our lives through the Holy Spirit.

This isn't a happiness that we can manufacture or pretend. It's a natural emotion flowing within the new disciple who's certain he/she has been forgiven and reconciled to God.

The external expression of that happiness will depend on our personality. For David, it was to write songs of praise to God. Those of us who like to sing aloud can identify with David. Others may not express it in an audible way but still praise God in their hearts.

....o **Ask the students to complete Activity 1.**

2. A HEART FULL OF GRATITUDE

In the Hebrew language, the words "praise" and "gratitude" come from the same root (yadah). The Bible is full of expressions of gratitude to God and words that encourage us to be grateful. But this attitude of thanks comes from a heart that has humbled itself before God and has recognized that everything it has, everything that is, and everything that will come into its life in the future, comes from God.

Jesus taught us to pray for things as simple as the daily bread, or the food that sustains us. This is a giant change in the way of thinking. A self-centered heart aims at achievements, but the God-centered heart recognizes that every great or small thing that happens in our lives has been provided by our Lord.

Gratitude should then always be something normal in the life of one who has been saved by the grace of Jesus. However, it doesn't always flow naturally because our human nature tends to take credit for the gains obtained by attributing them to personal effort. That's why the Word often reminds us that we should be grateful and praise God in everything.

||| **Ask a student to read 1 Thessalonians 5:18.** |||

............o **Ask the students to share their experiences as indicated in Activity 2.**

3. SOMEONE WHO CRIES OUT FOR FELLOWSHIP WITH GOD

To enjoy fellowship with the Creator is an enormous privilege enjoyed by all the sons and daughters of God. In the beginning, the new believers may have some misconceptions about how to talk to God. But little by little, they will understand that they can approach their Lord with all confidence, just as a little boy talks to his father. Over time, prayer becomes for the Christian something as natural as breathing.

We shouldn't expect the habit of prayer to arrive effortlessly on our part. Every Christian should discipline his/her life and set aside a quality time each day to speak with his/her Lord. That time will depend on the time of day when we can find a space of stillness and which is best to focus on God and His Word.

The Holy Spirit within us makes us want those "conversations" with God, makes us yearn to know more and more of Him, and the best way to get to know him is to speak with Him. It's difficult to express this longing with words, so the psalmist compares it to thirst. In Psalm 42:1-2 it says: *"As the deer pants for streams of water, so my soul pants for you, my God. My soul thirsts for God, for the living God. When can I go and meet with God?"* This insatiable thirst for fellowship with God is one of the fruits of this new life as the son or daughter of God.

The Lord Jesus Christ is our best model of a life of prayer. He prayed when he was happy and when he was sad. When he was relaxed and when he was stressed. Fatigue never stopped him from praying. Sometimes he spent all night praying (Luke 6:12).

Developing a discipline of prayer and being sensitive to that thirst of our soul for fellowship with God is indispensable for our permanence in the way of the Lord.

4. Desire to be with the family of God

||| Ask a student to read Ephesians 2:19 and another 1 Peter 2:9-10. |||

Christians are members of the family of God. This is what the Apostle Peter says in 1 Peter 2:9-10. We're a "chosen people." We belong to a family. All who have accepted Christ as their Lord and Savior belong to the family of God. The church has been chosen by God to be his special family.

Every new believer needs the love and warmth of this family to be able to survive - spiritually speaking - in this sin-polluted world. This sharing among Christians is also called "fellowship."

At the beginning of the Christian life, it's normal to feel afraid to enter a group of people that we don't know. But soon, when we begin to make friends, we begin to want to be in fellowship with the "brothers and sisters in Christ". In the Family of God, Christ is the elder brother, and we are all members of the same family (Romans 8:29). With the passing of time, we'll come to love the family of faith as if it were our blood family. This is no accident; God is preparing us to live for all eternity with our spiritual family.

In the local church, new believers or spiritual babies should receive love, warmth, instruction, protection and discipline. One of the ways human beings learn is by imitation, and only by being with the church can we learn to live as sons and daughters of God. The church must live as a family where the members care and help one another (Galatians 6:10).

However, we shouldn't expect the church to be "perfect." While it's true that the church must live in holiness, at the same time, the church is composed of human beings who are different in many ways and are the fruit of the religious, social, political, cultural and economic influences they have received from their families. Many times, this causes friction and differences of opinion in the family of God. Nevertheless, in a family, love and respect must prevail. In God's family, we must put all our effort into understanding, loving and supporting each other, which is how families stay together and are stronger.

·····················o **Complete Activity 3.**

5. A REFOCUSED VISION

What makes a man or a woman change how they live?

In the Bible, in the history of the Church and around us, we find thousands of examples of how Jesus Christ transforms lives.

[[[Ask two volunteers to read the passages of Luke 5:10-11 and Matthew 9:9.]]]

For example, in Luke 5:10-11, we see how the lives of several fishermen were changed, the product of a miracle in a day of fishing. In fact, the passage says, *"So they pulled their boats up on shore, left everything and followed him"* and they began to be disciples of Jesus. We also have the example of Matthew when he was sitting collecting taxes. Suddenly Jesus appeared, looked at him and said, *"Follow me"* (Matthew 9:9) and the Word says, *"Matthew got up and followed him."* The life of these men changed in an instant.

Our vision of the world around us changes when the Spirit of God comes to dwell in our lives. Before, we saw the world, people and ourselves with our own eyes. But now, we begin to see around us with the eyes of Jesus. As we become more acquainted with Jesus and relate to Him and His Word, our vision is refocused so that we can see how Jesus sees.

·····················o **We see an example in Activity 4.**

The new life in Christ brings with it a refocusing of our way of seeing people, of ordering our priorities, of our use of time and of how we use money, among others issues.

This refocusing of life isn't a cosmetic change that affects only the exterior of our life, nor is it striving to obey certain rules, but a transformation from the inside out, which is initiated by a change of motivations and feelings, and can be seen by others in the way we live our lives.

6. REJECTION OF ALL KINDS OF SIN

For the child of God, the way to face the problems of life and personal conflicts is based on the principles of the Word of God and love. Christians cannot continue to solve problems like they used to when they lived in sin.

People without Christ solve their problems by using coercion, violence, manipulation, lying, authoritarianism, shouting, anger, rude words, and many other forms of sin. Christians, on the contrary, follow the example and teaching of Jesus.

[[[Ask a student to read Ephesians 4:22-32.]]]

When the Christian is faced with a situation of how he may have acted before (lying, manipulating or otherwise) something different happens in his life. A voice inside him reprimands him, makes him feel sadness for what he has done or how he has done it.

[[[Ask the students: Whose voice is it according to verse 30?]]]

The presence of the Holy Spirit in our lives makes us different. We can no longer sin with freedom as we once did. The Word of God says that the Spirit that dwells in us is grieved when we sin.

Ask the class to complete Activity 5.

In the Bible, we find clear examples of how a heart transformed by the power of God seeks to resolve difficult circumstances according to the Word of God. In Acts 6:1-7, there was a problem that arose in the Jerusalem church that could have sparked a serious conflict. The apostles solved it by opening space for others to participate in the ministry. Thus, the apostles continued to fulfill their calling and the widows would continue to be served in their needs. The principle that helped them to solve the problem was the need to seek the good for all involved.

In Galatians 6:1, we find another problem. This was a case of a brother who had sinned and the church had to make a decision on the matter. The apostle Paul advises that when someone is caught in a sin, those who are spiritual must seek to restore him by helping him to carry his burden or his shame. This, by the way, isn't the most simple or easy solution. Humanly, when someone betrays us, we want to make him pay for what he did to us. But the attitude of Christ towards the sinner is one of forgiving love that seeks to restore, and this is the path that Paul tells them to take. The principle here is to love and forgive those who disappoint us, even if this is very hard to do.

In Galatians 2:11, we find a problem of conflict between two brothers in the faith, both leaders in the church. Paul had realized that Peter was misbehaving toward non-Jewish believers. Instead of beginning to criticize Peter behind his back, he preferred to talk about it face to face. What a great example for the church! The Bible doesn't tell us that this incident affected in any way their relationship. On the contrary, Peter corrected his attitude and both leaders continued to spread the gospel. The principle here is that to resolve interpersonal conflicts, the best way is to confront each other and speak the truth with love, always seeking the good and growth of our brother or sister.

Definition of key terms

- **Praise:** Verbal expressions that come spontaneously from the heart of the person in recognition of who God is.

- **Fellowship:** This relationship among believers is also known by the Greek term "koinonia." The term was used extensively in the New Testament to describe the church at that time. Koinonia is love that unites believers in Christ. Koinonía is possible when the brothers in the Faith possess the Holy Spirit in their hearts and they practice the sacraments together like, for example, the Lord's Supper.

Summary

The experience of salvation is something which is worked out within the heart, but can be seen by external changes in the Christian's life. Salvation - when it's true - can be seen by other people through the "fruits of repentance" shown in every aspect of the new disciple's life.

Activity Worksheet

ACTIVITY 1

How do you express in your life the joy of being a Christian? Which of these Bible examples do you identify with? Search in your Bible for some different expressions of inner happiness that are similar to your experience. Then compare them with the rest of the class

Psalms 32:11 _____

Psalms 92: 2 _____

Ephesians 5:19 _____

Other _____

ACTIVITY 2

Respond to the following questions and then share your answers with the rest of the class.

1. What dangers might occur when a Christian fails to be grateful?

_____

_____

2. How can we practically demonstrate our gratitude to God?

_____

_____

3. What changes can we make in our lives to learn to be more grateful?

_____

_____

ACTIVITY 3

In groups of 3-4, read Acts 2:42-47 and make a list of the things that the members of the first church in Jerusalem did together. Then in the right column make a list of those things you do together in your local church. Finally, notice the coincidences and discuss them.

How did the church in Jerusalem cultivate fellowship?	How do we develop our fellowship?
_____	_____
_____	_____
_____	_____
_____	_____
_____	_____

_____   _____

_____   _____

_____   _____

_____   _____

Discuss among one another: In our local church, are we giving evidence that we are one family in Christ? Is there anything else we should do to strengthen the bonds of brotherhood between us?

ACTIVITY 4.
Have you ever had any of these experiences? Mark with a "yes" those that you have experienced in your life.

__ Walk down a street with so many people that you almost cannot move forward.

__ Have a panoramic view of a city from a high place.

__ Look out the window when the plane lands to see the city.

__ Be at the exit of the subway at rush hour.

__ Travel in a train or bus full of people.

__ Get stuck with your car in traffic for hours.

__ Stand in the line for the supermarket or bank for much longer than usual

If your answer is yes, remember what you thought, said or felt at that moment. Then ask yourself, did I think, say, or feel something like this ... , and mark "yes" in the list below that applies.

__ What a nuisance! Where did all these people come from?

__ What a disgrace that in this city there is no place for even one person!

__ What bad luck, I should have left early!

__ When will the government do something to fix this chaos?

__ Another reaction: _____

Now reflect for a few moments: How different would your reaction have been if you had looked at that city or the crowd with the eyes of Jesus?

_____

_____

Finally, compare your answer with Matthew 9:36, and share your answers with the rest of the class.

_____

_____

ACTIVITY 5.
Reflect on the following story and respond to the questions at the end.

A young Christian woman who was looking for work was recommended by a brother of the church to work in a friend's toy store. It was a large business that sold toys for small toy stores. The first day she showed up in the morning and went to the accounting office where they explained to her what her responsibilities were as an administrative assistant. Among other things, she was taught to write checks and them register in the accounting books. She began to work with much enthusiasm. The salary they offered was not large, but it wasn't bad either.

However, something strange happened very soon after she had started. The treasurer explained that there were two books to register the checks, and that she would be told which book to register the cash in. Then the explanation continued: "This book is the one that we show if the tax inspectors come from the government, and this one we keep hidden here. This we call the black book."

The girl understood the explanation clearly and returned to her chair. But something began to happen in her mind and heart. A voice inside her told her that that was wrong, that if she stayed in this job, she would be forced to lie. The young woman apologized to the treasurer and said, "Excuse me, I need this job and you have been very kind to me, but I cannot stay. If I do what you tell me, I would have to hide data and the government would be defrauded. As a Christian, I cannot do this. Please understand the reasons why I cannot accept this job." She left the business and never came back.

1. Do you think that the girl made the right decision?

_____

_____

2. What impact do you think her behavior had on the treasurer?

_____

_____

3. Do you know anyone who is currently in a similar situation? If so, what would be your advice for this person?

_____

_____

_____

RECOMMENDED READINGS

- *Psalm 92*
- *Psalm 148*
- *2 Corinthians 6*
- *Ephesians 4:17-32.*
- *Ephesians 5:1-20*

Sinful attitudes that need to be cleansed
Lesson 6

Learning goals:

That the students ...

- Get to know the sinful attitudes that remained in the disciples that Jesus had to rebuke.
- Compare their own attitudes with those of the disciples.
- Share their testimonies about these sinful attitudes that are present in their lives which need to be dealt with.
- Understand that we must be patient with one other while discovering the areas of our lives that need to be purified and delivered to the Lord.

Resources

- Pieces of cardboard with the following words written on them: doubt, selfishness, impatience, anger, intolerance, pride, bad temper, vindictiveness, aggression, ambition for power; Sticky tape to stick the pieces of cardboard onto the blackboard. Another option is write the words on the board. If you can, use colors.

Introduction

By looking at the gigantic work done by the Apostles recorded for us in the book of Acts and other New Testament books, we may easily want to conclude that these were extraordinary men with few weaknesses. However, if we look carefully, they don't appear to be the same men who were with Jesus as portrayed in the Gospels.

The truth is that Jesus chose twelve imperfect men who needed to be changed. When Jesus called them, they didn't appear to be very spiritual or intellectual. They were impulsive (John 21:7; 13:9; 9:54; 1 John 4:8); sinners (Mark 9:33-34; 10:37; Luke 22:24); incapable of solving many problems (Matthew 18:21-35, 9:3, Luke 10:29, 20:22); ignorant and biased (Mark 10:22) and unstable in their faith (John 6:67). None of Jesus' disciples "belonged to the upper classes. They were fishermen, tax collectors, working men. Matthew and Simon the Zealot were even, because of their adhesions, political enemies."[2]

What did Jesus make of this group of men with so many imperfections? "Judging by the results, the best generation of teachers the world has known: twelve men who later revolutionized the world." It has been said: "The greatest miracle in history seems to be the transformation that Jesus effected in those men." [4]

Jesus chose imperfect people who recognized their need to be changed. Other people in Jesus' time needed to be renewed, but they didn't recognize Him, like the Pharisees whom He condemned for their vanity and pride, because they refused to admit their sin and consequent need of being changed.

The purpose of this lesson is to study some of the sinful attitudes that came to light in the lives of the disciples and how Jesus corrected them, so that we can examine our lives to discover and identify those attitudes rooted in the depths of our heart that aren't in keeping with the holy life that God wants us to live.

[1] Price, J.M. *Jesus the Teacher.* El Paso, Texas: CPB, s/f. pp. 29-46.

[2] Gabner-Hainer, A. *Practical Vocabulary of the Bible.* Barcelona: Herder, 1975, p. 407.

[3] Maquis cited in Price, Op. cit. p. 46.

[4] T. R. Glover cited in Price, Op. cit. p. 45.

Bible Study

As they walked along with Jesus, the disciples demonstrated that there were things that were difficult for them to accept. They wanted to be like Jesus, but found in themselves thoughts and ideas that contradicted his teachings, revealing a root of selfishness in their hearts. We must thank God for the writers of the Gospels because they didn't hide the spiritual struggles that the disciples had in trying to live a life of holiness and behaving as Jesus expected them to. Let's see if there are attitudes such as these that get in the way of us living our lives in a way that reflects Jesus.

1. THEY DOUBTED, THEIR FAITH WAS WEAK

||| Write on the board the definition of faith that is included in the definition of terms. |||

o Ask a student to read Matthew 8:23-27. Then ask the students to complete Activity 1 in groups of 3. Then ask them to continue by completing Activity 2 alone.

There comes a time in the life of every Christian that faith has to be tested. It's something that happens to the majority of the young Christians when they study at university where they hear many "voices" that may question and deny the truthfulness of the existence of God, of Jesus and the validity of the Bible as authority for life.

Today, these voices reach out to Christians of all ages through the media. Almost every day we are exposed to information that contradicts and denies the Bible's claims about the origin of human beings, about the reality of a God who loves us and relates to us and has a purpose for our life. They question the existence of sin, of Jesus ... and even of ourselves!

A weak faith will not survive this storm of lies. A doubting Christian is vulnerable to temptation, and at any moment he can fall back into sin. Every believer must decide whether to believe God, whom he cannot see, or believe what he sees and hears in the mass media outlets. Faith is developed by the Holy Spirit in our lives, but it depends on us to decide that we want to grow and become strong.

||| Draw a large enough heart on the board so that all the words on the cards will fit into it. Stick in the word 'Doubt'. As the lesson unfolds, other words will be added to the heart. |||

2. THEY FOCUSED ON HUMAN THINGS

One of the harshest reprimands Jesus gave his disciples was addressed to Peter.

||| Read Mark 8:31-37. |||

This moment related by Mark took place in one of Jesus' private lessons to his group of disciples. On this occasion, the Master told them about the events that would surround his death and resurrection. Peter removed Jesus from the group and tried to dissuade him from these pessimistic thoughts. Jesus' reacted immediately addressing the whole group, and he rebuked

Peter in front of them with these words, *"Get behind me, Satan! ... You don't have in mind the concerns of God, but merely human concerns."*

Why did Jesus speak to Peter in this way by calling him Satan? The answer is simple. Peter thought that he was fulfilling his duty as a representative of the group, trying to convince Jesus not to take the road that would lead to his death. As a human being, his mind told him that it's reasonable to flee from suffering. But his thoughts were far from the will of God, and his words had the same intention as the words of Satan when he tempted Jesus in the desert, trying to detour him from the mission for which he had come to this world.

It wasn't that Peter was consciously letting himself be used by Satan, but his thoughts were impregnated by this world's selfish way of thinking. This way of thinking is normal for people who live without God, but it's almost always opposed to the truth of God and His will for our lives.

In the following verse, Jesus makes one of the most important and most talked about statements in the history of the Church, stating that no one can be his disciple if he is not willing to take up the cross and follow him. For us today, taking the cross means to be willing to obey God in whatever he asks us to do to carry salvation to this lost world. Carrying His cross implies deciding to give everything for His cause -whatever it takes- even giving our own lives for Him.

The disciples had not yet fully and totally given their lives to the Lord.

··o **Ask the students to complete Activity 3.**

3. THEY BECAME IMPATIENT AND UPSET WITH PEOPLE

||| **Ask a student to read Matthew 19:13-15.** |||

It seems that humans always demands patience for themselves, but have problems being patient with others. It's especially difficult for adults to be patient with children.

The disciples were bothered by the parents who took their little children to Jesus to bless. The Jews had a habit of blessing children by placing their hands on their heads. This was a form of dedication or consecration to God, and from that point forward, the person was considered to belong to God.

Jesus rebuked the disciples' attitude because of how they acted. Urging the children to go away from Jesus was tantamount to discriminating against the children, closing the door for divine grace and salvation.

Impatience leads to **anger**, and anger leads us to sin. Impatience arises from **intolerance** or lack of acceptance of other people. Christians must be people who love others as they are, and not only when they like how other folk are or how they behave. This love can only be received from God when pride has been cleansed from our heart.

4. THEY SHOWED HARDNESS IN JUDGING OTHERS

||| **Ask a student to read Luke 9:51-54.** |||

On this occasion, the people of this village in Samaria had been rude to Jesus by denying him the help he had requested. Jews and Samaritans hated each other and Jesus had to pass through the land of Samaria to reach Jerusalem. Probably the disciples feared that thieves would assault them and hurt the Master.

James and John (who were nicknamed the 'sons of thunder') felt offended by these Samaritans, and full of national pride, they ask Jesus for permission to send fire from heaven to consume the city and its people. Again, there was impatience coupled with **vindictiveness** or lack of mercy, and a desire for **revenge**.

God will never place His authority and power at our disposal so that we may punish others for having offended our **pride**. James and John wanted to use the power of God to satisfy their desire for revenge. This attitude of the apostles reminds us of the prophet Jonah, who sat down to wait for God to destroy the city. It never occurred to him for a moment to realize that God's not a vengeful God, but one that views all nations with mercy.

Jesus rebukes them harshly because their thoughts and their desires were diametrically opposed to the heart of God. James and John had a heart full of bitterness against the Samaritans. They were more worried about the offense they had received that had hurt their pride than in showing the Samaritans the love of God.

Their reaction to the aggression of the enemies didn't correspond to the "Spirit of Jesus." They continued to react in these circumstances in ways which weren't worthy of a son or daughter of God.

Letting feelings of hatred, bitterness, and desires of revenge take root in our hearts is contrary to the love and mercy of Christ that must fill us.

Guide the students to complete Activity 4.

5. THEY FOUGHT TO DEFEND THEIR RIGHTS TO BE THE FIRST

[[[Ask a volunteer to read Luke 22:24-30.]]]

This event that Luke relates occurs during the last supper, hours before Jesus was arrested. It wasn't the first time the disciples had a similar discussion (Matthew 18:1-5, Mark 10:35-45). In their hearts, they were willing to **fight**, and in this case wanted to resolve who deserved the right to be the leader. Although he doesn't tell us who was involved in the discussion, we can assume that it was between Peter, James and John, three disciples who **aspired** to a place of leadership.

It's interesting that Jesus doesn't prevent them from getting into a heated discussion, probably because he was absorbed in His own thoughts reflecting on the events ahead. But most likely, Jesus hoped that one of them would remember his teachings about loving our neighbors. But this didn't happen. They were too engrossed by their desire to win the argument. Unable to reach an agreement, they returned to Jesus to see who was right.

Jesus' response, far from being what they expected, leads them to reflect on the motives that led them to want to be spiritual leaders. Jesus makes it clear that leadership in the church is not the same as what we are accustomed to seeing in this world.

In the first place, Jesus said that they must not serve others in order to lord it over them. In this case Jesus cited an example of the kings of that time who were accustomed to dividing their conquered lands among his soldiers and these in turn in gratitude told the world of their benefactor.

Many want to have positions of leadership because it represents an opportunity for others to obey them, and they want to receive words of praise, which feed the inner desire to feel important, to want to excel over others, to fatten one's pride.

Jesus makes it clear that this type of leadership is easy and doesn't deserve any reward from God. As leaders, Christians should not seek position, fame, power, honors or material reward from the people they serve, but seek to please God first, adopting the attitude of a servant.

The spiritual leaders that Jesus can use to guide his people are those who renounce pride and are humble, getting alongside the needy in order to serve them. The authority that God delegates to his leaders is that of a servant not seeking to be one above the rest.

6. THEY HAD DIFFICULTY SERVING THEIR NEIGHBORS WITH HUMILITY

||| Ask a student to read John 13:1-5. |||

This event occurs shortly before Jesus' death. Verse 1 tells us that Jesus knew that the hour of his death had come. All the time that Jesus Christ lived as a man and served in this world, he knew that He was walking towards his destination - the cross. The Son of God had come into the world to reach that moment that was the supreme goal of his coming, to give himself up as a sacrifice for our sins.

But on this occasion, we find Jesus giving a very important lesson to the disciples. In those times, people moved from one place to another walking on dusty roads, wearing sandals tied with leather straps that covered their feet. Thus, their feet were often dusty and uncomfortable. Arriving at a house, the good host had a slave wash the feet of the guests as a gesture of welcome. The disciples were in a borrowed room in which there was no host, and although the water and the towel were there, none of the twelve took the initiative to wash the tired feet. No one wanted to take the place of a servant.

Probably everyone was waiting for Jesus to point to one of them and order them to do it. While they were eating, Jesus stood up in silence, took the water, and began to wash their feet. Jesus, the Son of God incarnate, didn't feel that assuming this work to serve other people was a dishonor or a humiliation, but the pride that was rooted in the disciples' hearts made them think differently.

||| Ask a volunteer to read verses 6 -11 of John 13. Then ask the students: Why do you think Peter reacted in this way? |||

In verse 7, Jesus gives us the answer. Peter could not understand that Jesus, the leader of the group, the Son of God, God made flesh, was reduced to taking the role of a slave, which was considered to be a job of the lowest strata of society. But Jesus told him that they might not understand at that moment what He was doing, but later on, it would become clear to them.

What does Jesus mean by this? When would Peter understand that serving one's neighbor doesn't degrade us in the eyes of God, but quite the opposite?

||| Ask a student to read verses 12-20. |||

It's clear in these words of Jesus that serving others should be a natural characteristic in the life of the Christian. Although the disciples loved the Lord and wanted to imitate Him in everything He did, they still didn't quite understand the greatness of His love, and weren't able to love others in this way; they couldn't live life like Jesus yet.

While Jesus was with them, He was the model of that kind of life where the love of God is poured out from the Heart. They were with Him and saw this over and over again, but they weren't able to reproduce this holy love in their own lives. Jesus knew this. The love of God cannot be imitated or obtained by human efforts. It doesn't come through making personal sacrifices, or by being convinced that's what must be done.

In verse 20, he tells them that the ability to love in this way could only come into their lives when they receive the One he would send in His place. In chapter 14:16-17, Jesus tells them that He'll send the Holy Spirit. This work of the Holy Spirit will be the subject of the next lesson.

Ask the students to complete Activity 5.

In the next lesson, we'll talk about the provision that God has made through the death of Christ, and the work of the Spirit in our life, freeing us from these selfish attitudes (point to the heart on the board) that get in the way of the love of Jesus from taking over our spirit, mind and heart.

Ask the students to complete Activity 6. Then conclude with a time of individual prayer.

Definition of key terms

- **Faith:** Faith comes from the Greek word "pistis" which means "to be convinced, to believe strongly, and to have the conviction that a thing is real, true or certain."

- **Servant:** A servant is one who works for another person. Servants can be slaves or can be paid for their services. In saying that we are servants of God, we're saying that He is our Owner and we're at His disposal.

- **Slave:** A slave is that person who serves someone because that other person is the owner of their life. Slaves almost always have few or no rights, and can be used by their master or owner in the way they please. Being a slave is the exact opposite of being a free person. But sometimes, by our own decision, we can decide to become slaves for someone. This happens when we decided to become servants of God; we're saying that we want to be His slaves so He can control our lives.

- **Humility:** Humility implies having a modest or low view of one's own importance. In order to be humble, we must understand that our own pride can lead us to have a much higher self-concept of who we really are. Although many times we are successful and prosperous, as humble people we have to understand that everything we have, including our lives, is a gift of the grace of God.

- **Selfishness:** The Word of God tells us in Matthew 10:8b: *"Freely you have received; freely give."* When we don't want to carry out this command given by our Lord Jesus Christ, we're being selfish, not wanting others to have what we have.

- **Pride:** When we refer to pride, we mean that arrogance, vanity and excessive self-esteem are part of our lives.

Summary

The passages studied show us some of the reactions that came to light in the life of the Disciples where there is evidence that they needed a deeper cleansing work of getting rid of the sin in their lives. Following Jesus and serving others requires that these attitudes be purified.

Every Christian, as well as those disciples, has negative thoughts, attitudes, words, and even actions. Only the power of the Holy Spirit dwelling fully in the believer can cleanse this undesirable sin that brings sadness and pain to whoever wants to please God and obey him fully in thought, word and action.

Activity Worksheet

ACTIVITY 1

In groups of 3 or 4, read Matthew 8:23-27 and answer the following questions:

1. Why did Jesus rebuke the disciples on this occasion?

_____

2. What were they afraid of?

_____

3. What did they doubt?

_____

4. Do you agree that fear and doubt are symptoms of a lack of faith?

_____

5. Write some ideas about what faith is.

_____

_____

6. Read 2 Timothy 1:12 and compare what you said about faith from the definition on the board and the ideas you wrote about it in the previous question. Then write a group definition of faith.

_____

_____

7. Based on these definitions, describe what weak faith is. (You can use words like: suspicious, doubtful, fearful, fluctuating, undecided and others).

_____

_____

ACTIVITY 2

Mark in the chart below a number between 0 and 10 in each category on how your faith is at this time? Circle the number, with 0 being the lowest and 10 being the highest.

1.	Weak	0-1-2-3-4-5-6-7-8-9-10	Strong
2.	Distrustful	0-1-2-3-4-5-6-7-8-9-10	Trustful
3.	I find it hard to believe	0-1-2-3-4-5-6-7-8-9-10	I find it easy to believe

4.	Impatient	0-1-2-3-4-5-6-7-8-9-10	Patient
5.	I frequently doubt.	0-1-2-3-4-5-6-7-8-9-10	I never doubt.
6.	I believe if I see the evidence.	0-1-2-3-4-5-6-7-8-9-10	I believe even if I can't see.
7.	I doubt the promises of God.	0-1-2-3-4-5-6-7-8-9-10	I believe in God's promises.
8.	It makes no difference in my life.	0-1-2-3-4-5-6-7-8-9-10	It helps me live.
9.	I don't believe in miracles.	0-1-2-3-4-5-6-7-8-9-10	I pray for and expect miracles.
10.	I am afraid for my future.	0-1-2-3-4-5-6-7-8-9-10	I trust my future to God.

ACTIVITY 3
Read Mark 8:34 and respond:

a. Do you have, or have you had, trouble following Jesus, or obeying everything he asks of you?

_____

b. What has been or is your greatest obstacle to following Jesus?

_____

c. What are you willing to do to follow Jesus today, if he asked you?

Mark NO, MAYBE, or YES in the next list.

	No	Maybe	Yes
1. Risk your life preaching in a country where there's the death penalty for becoming a Christian.	_____	_____	_____
2. Care for a sick person with AIDS.	_____	_____	_____
3. Go as a missionary to a country where you can get sick of something incurable.	_____	_____	_____
4. Go and evangelize children in a neighborhood where there are violent gangs.	_____	_____	_____
5. Spend sleepless nights caring for recovering drug addicts.	_____	_____	_____
6. Sell your comfortable car to buy an old minibus and bring people to church.	_____	_____	_____
7. Sacrifice the time of sports games to prepare to teach others.	_____	_____	_____

	No	Maybe	Yes
8. Give up a well-paying job to have more time for ministry.	_____	_____	_____
9. Give money to missions instead of fast food that you like.	_____	_____	_____
10. Sleep less to study at the seminary or school of leadership.	_____	_____	_____

ACTIVITY 4.

Reflect and then share with the rest of the class.

1. When was the last time you lost your temper and became angry?

_____

2. What was the reason? What bothered you?

_____

3. Did this anger lead you to do something you now regret?

_____

4. Do you think your reaction is due to pride, vanity, selfishness or self-indulgence in your heart?

_____

5. Do you think you would be a better Christian if your heart were free from these selfish tendencies?

_____

ACTIVITY 5.

Respond to the following questions:

1. Why is it so difficult for us to serve others?

_____

2. What are the service jobs to others or to the community that are less valued by society?

_____

3. How would you feel doing one of these jobs?

_____

4. Make a list of those things in which it costs you to serve others with a good spirit in your home, in your work, in the church, in your community, etc.

_____

_____

_____

5. What do you think you need to have in order to be willing to serve others like Jesus did?

_____

ACTIVITY 6.

Draw a picture that represents your heart and write in it the sinful attitudes which are present in your life that need to be changed.

Then take time privately to pray, asking God to help you understand how to be free from all of that.

RECOMMENDED READINGS

- John 1:19-28
- John 14:15-31
- John 15:1-17
- John 16:1-24
- John 17:1-26.

Natural, carnal or spiritual?
Lesson 7

Learning goals:

That the students ...

- Know the different spiritual states and the biblical language that describes them.
- Understand that the Christian hasn't been saved to live as a slave to sin.
- Identify where their lives are right now in terms of their spiritual progress.
- Be aware that the fullness of the Spirit isn't an option but a further stage in a Christian's development.
- Be encouraged to experience that quality life, free from sin, which the fullness of the Spirit makes possible.

Resources

- Candies, blackboard, markers or chalk to write on blackboard

Introduction

In the previous lesson, we studied about the sinful attitudes that remain in believers, and are the fruit of the root of sin that nests in our inner beings. In this lesson and the next one, we'll study four types of spiritual states, and we'll know more about the sin that dwells in the life of the believer and that hinders him from living according to the will of God.

Ask the students to complete Activity 1. Then ask them to say with whom they identify the most. For example: Who identifies themselves with Julie? Who with Mike? And so on. Then congratulate your class for their honesty and give them some candy as a reward for a job well done.

Continue to explain the next part of the lesson, and as you speak, write the characters' names and the keyword for each on the blackboard.

For those who identified with Julie, the keyword describing her experience with God is 'relationship.' Congratulate those students and tell them that they're spiritual people. Their spiritual development is as it should be.

If their life is like Mike's, the keyword is 'dissatisfaction.' They must not be discouraged. Now they know God, but want more, and that sense of dissatisfaction is one more stage of Christian growth. This feeling that something is missing is a sign that the Holy Spirit is working, because God wants to bring them to a more complete surrender to His will. Congratulate this group of students and tell them that they're on the right track.

For those whose life resembles Karen, the keyword that describes her experience with God is 'religion'. Those people in this group are 'natural people', that is, they haven't yet accepted Christ as their personal Savior.

For those who stated that their life is similar to Henry, the keyword describing their experience with God is 'knowing'; and in the words of the apostle Paul, they're called 'carnal Christians.' Their lives aren't what God wants for them. They need a deeper commitment to the Lord.

Bible Study

Every Christian who wishes to grow to become like Christ goes through these three stages in their spiritual lives:

1. ONE WHO WALKS IN SIN (NATURAL PERSON)

||| Ask for two volunteers to read Ephesians 2:1-3 and Galatians 5:19-21. |||

The natural person is like Karen, who's alive physically but spiritually dead because she lives apart from God. Her mind, emotions and will are directed by her own desires. She makes decisions guided by her own understanding without seeking for God's guidance in the Word of God. We studied this spiritual state in the first lessons of this quarter.

In Ephesians, we read that all who are now saved went through this stage when we lived in disobedience to God. This is a person who commits sin in thought, in speech and in actions. The list of sins in Galatians 5 includes both inner sins and external manifestations that can be seen, that are the fruit of those other sins that cannot be seen.

The natural person is spiritually dead. They can be very evil people or even good, decent citizens who see themselves as good, but don't have Christ in their lives. They don't have the Spirit, nor eternal life. They have bodies and souls, but no spiritual life. Romans 8:9 says, *"You, however, aren't in the realm of the flesh but are in the realm of the Spirit, if indeed the Spirit of God lives in you. And if anyone doesn't have the Spirit of Christ, they don't belong to Christ."*

People like Karen needs to repent of their sins and accept Christ as their personal Savior.

2. THE BELIEVER WHO FOLLOWS CHRIST BUT IS STILL IN THE FLESH (CARNAL PERSON)

When we're born again, the Holy Spirit comes to dwell in our being and initiates a process of transformation which lasts throughout our lifetime. We're new people, born again as sons and daughters of God. We enjoy a new way of life, but as Mike soon discovered, it wasn't quite as good as he expected.

||| Ask a student to read Galatians 5:16-17. |||

All Christians live in the flesh, because we're in a body of flesh. But there's a big difference between living and following the desires of the flesh. This Greek word that is translated "flesh" represents everything that opposes the Holy Spirit. The desires of the flesh make us serve the flesh; in other words, to follow our own inclinations whether they be in our body, mind or emotions. It isn't that out bodies are essentially bad, for God created us, and all things that He made are good and useful. But the problem is that we've gotten used to satisfying ourselves in selfish ways.

For example, an alcoholic who wants to stop drinking finds it hard not to listen to how his body craves alcohol, making him drink more and thus becoming dependent on alcohol. Unless his will can overwhelm his physical desires, he may very well remain an alcoholic for life.

Now, this selfish side remains in all new believers, and very soon manifests itself in the life of the disciple as we saw in the previous lesson. Some Christians are confused when they discover this longing within themselves to return to the things they have left, comes back. This is probably because they thought that when they accepted Jesus as their savior, that was the end of all problems with sin. However, this doesn't happen. In fact, a kind of war begins inside us. We're tempted and it's hard to overcome those temptations, because there's an increasing desire within us to satisfy our selfish nature, which is opposed to the life that Jesus wants us to lead.

This inner force that invites us to desire the opposite of the will of God is also known as the "old nature", or the "old man." This desire comes from the root of Adam's sin with which the whole human race has been contaminated. This "old self" wants new Christians to go back to the customs they had before, and fights against the new habits of praying, tithing, loving enemies, serving others first, etc. The body and mind of new Christians resist changes; they don't want to separate from the old friends.

Someone described the Christian's life at this stage as having two lions fighting inside to see who can be in charge. One is the old lion, our old will also called the old man or the selfish "I", accustomed to dominating and having no intention of subjecting itself to Christ. This is our old identity, our old life accustomed to sin, what we were before we were born again. The other lion is young. It is the new life, the regenerated and reborn person in Christ who wishes to please his Savior and Lord. The believer soon discovers that the old lion is difficult to keep under control.

Christians aren't supposed to remain a long time in this state. In the following lessons, we'll see the solution God has provided in Christ to enable us to have complete freedom from this condition of sin.

3. THE BELIEVER WHO LIVES THE LIFE OF CHRIST (SPIRITUAL PERSON)

||| Ask a student to read Romans 8:1. |||

There's another way of living that God wanted for us since he gave us life in Christ Jesus. This is the life according to the Spirit. Like Julie, the spiritual person has gone beyond the experience of salvation and has discovered that being filled with the Spirit has changed his/her life.

As we read the first chapters of the book of Acts, we'll see that when the disciples were filled with the Holy Spirit, there was a wonderful change in their lives. While they were with Jesus, they weren't able to live the life that Jesus wanted for them. But when the Spirit filled them, they suddenly began to have power to be able to live in victory as the Lord desired for them.

Let's look at some of the results of the fullness of the Spirit in the lives of those men and women.

Their relationship with Jesus was different

While the disciples walked with Jesus, they couldn't have him inside their hearts. Jesus was with them, but still his teachings didn't seem to take root in their hearts. He taught them about humility and about the danger of feeling greater than other people, and yet they fought amongst themselves about which of them was greater.

It wasn't until Christ was able to enter into them through the Holy Spirit that he could master the pride they had in their hearts. This was impossible before Jesus Christ gave his life so that sin could be totally cleansed from their lives. So it is with us, only by being filled with the Holy Spirit can we have Jesus Christ living in us.

||| Read John 14:23. |||

When the Spirit fills us, a new love for God takes root in our hearts. When we receive the love of God, it floods our being. It begins to overflow and we start loving other people. Our hearts are like a dam when the floodgates are opened and fresh water pours out into thirsty fields.

When Jesus fills us with life with His Spirit, we become one with him. It's something like a spiritual symbiosis. He begins to fill our thoughts with his thoughts, our affections with his own, and His passion becomes our passion. The normal thing in the Christian life is to want this deeper relationship with Jesus.

Strengthened unity in the Body of Christ

||| Ask a student to read Romans 5:5. |||

The love of God poured out in the hearts of the disciples replaces the bad attitudes that were there before. The love of God is what makes it possible for us to love other Christians and be willing to serve them in their needs. Christians in the early church shared their material goods and spiritual wealth.

Sometimes in the church, there are problems when people with different temperaments work together in the church. In some occasions, this may leads to in-fighting or divisions harming the fellowship. Each one says that they love God, but no one is willing to yield up their point of view to enable the work of God to continue. It's hard to believe that people like this are filled with this Spirit of God's love!

In our part of the world, there are still some buildings where clay was used to join stone blocks or adobes. These buildings have been maintained in some cases for more than a hundred years, but those walls are easy to demolish. In Spain, old houses can still be found in the villages, whose walls are of natural stones placed one on top of the other joined with mud. You can easily pull a small stone out of these walls because the mixture joining them isn't good. All these constructions were made where and when there was no cement available, or where it wasn't known that such a thing existed. But today, who would think of making a house by joining the bricks with mud?

God's love as described in the Bible is like the cement mixture used to attach the stones to a wall. This love is available. However, some continue to use substitutes that don't unite in the same way, like the mud that was used in the past.

Power to fulfill the mission entrusted to us by the Lord

||| Ask a student to read John 15:5. |||

The Spirit-filled believer has a special anointing that bears fruit when he/she serves the Lord. This is due to several factors, some of which we'll mention.

Spirit-filled Christians are humble to learn, and have died to the selfishness that led them to believe that they knew everything. People who study and prepare are more useful in the work of God, and their work yields more fruit. Others, because of pride, grope around making many mistakes that could be prevented, and spend their time and energy without much benefit.

Christians full of the Lord's presence work in partnership with the Holy Spirit. In their daily walk, they learn to converse with the Spirit and to make decisions guided by the Spirit. It is the Spirit who shows us where to go to preach the gospel. He reminds us of the teaching of the Word for every occasion, and He gives us practical wisdom to solve the problems of life and give advice to others.

The Holy Spirit goes before the spiritual person, preparing the hearts of the people so that they hunger to hear the Word of God and want to repent. The Holy Spirit also gives courage to the spiritual man or woman to speak to others without fear or shame.

Power to live in holiness

This experience is a second work of grace that gives us the power to live close to Christ and away from sin.

||| Ask a student to read Romans 6:11-14. |||

God's will for His children is that they shouldn't give sin any opportunity in their lives. He wants to express His love for this lost world through our whole being; to make our hands, minds and feet into useful and well-tuned instruments that He can use. Holy Christians speak truthfully, love righteousness, are passionate about God's work, and invest their time, abilities and possessions to serve God. The life of holiness is possible only when we're filled with the Holy Spirit of God.

4. THE CHRISTIAN WHO DOESN'T GROW (CARNAL CHRISTIAN)

The carnal person like Henry, though he has expressed his faith in Christ and is spiritually alive, prioritizes the things of this life over the spiritual ones. He often follows the impulses of the "flesh" guided by his appetites. The interests of this person and their decisions are self-centered. His mind is occupied by carnal thoughts. His emotions are dominated by negative feelings and his way of relating to God and with others manifest this inner imbalance.

||| Ask a volunteer to read James 1:8. |||

The apostle James calls him a "double minded man" or a person with divided loyalties. This person wants to live as a Christian and is worldly at the same time. He doesn't want to give up earthly pleasures, but he doesn't want to lose eternal life either.

People like these have their minds and their affections divided. They're not willing to give up their will to follow Christ one hundred percent. But the carnal Christian isn't living a life pleasing to Christ.

No son or daughter of God should remain in this double life. Sin is difficult to abandon. It penetrates our thinking and personality. It enslaves us, leading us to do things that embarrass us and prevent us from seeing the way God gives us through Jesus Christ. But every child of God can and should live free from the dominion of sin.

If we want God to completely remove sin from our lives and receive freedom from the power of sin, the next few lessons are going to go deeper into the danger of living in the flesh and the benefits of life in the Spirit.

Definition of key terms

- **Worldly:** belonging to the world, which serves sin and is opposed to God and His will. It can be used to refer to a custom, lifestyle or person who isn't pleasing to God.

- **Symbiosis:** association of two or more elements to form a single unit, a life in common.

- **Flesh:** the life of the person accustomed to sin whose lifestyle benefits their own selfish tastes, pleasures and ambitions. In this life, the "I" or the will of the person dominates.

- **Old nature, old way of life, old man:** ways of describing our life without Christ. It is called "old" to distinguish it from new life in Christ that has come to replace it.

Summary

All people live in one of the four spiritual states.

The natural person is one who doesn't have a relationship with God, lives in sin, has no spiritual life and unless he accepts Christ as Savior, is destined for hell.

The new Christian is a person who has been reborn by the Spirit and is in a stage of growth in his relationship with God. Following Jesus is made difficult by the inheritance of sin in our lives, and needs to be taken away by the Holy Spirit.

The spiritual person is one who has given one hundred percent of his life to the Lord, died to selfishness, and is growing in a loving relationship with Jesus and his/her fellow men.

Carnal Christians are believers who choose to live a double life, with one foot in the world and the other in the church. Their relationship with God isn't close, and their way of life isn't pleasing to God.

Activity Worksheet

ACTIVITY 1
Who do you identify with most? Which of these people represents your relationship with God, the world and your family?

Julie:

For Julie, God is a close and loving Father. This relationship is very important for her because both her father and the father of her children were not loving and tender people.

She enjoys her time alone with God, and talks to God as with a friend. She speaks of God with enthusiasm and is sure that God always listens to her, even when she is sad and discouraged. She speaks to God at home, while traveling to work, when she gets up, when she goes to bed, etc.... For her, God is the most interesting person in the universe, someone who is worth spending time to get to know more. For her, to obey God isn't a heavy burden, but is the natural response of someone who loves another and wants to please him.

Julie has given God control over her whole life and always asks him how to use her talents, how to educate her children, and every important and small decision of her life is under His guidance.

For Julie, to live every day in this world confronts her with a great challenge. She knows that the customs of the people and the principles by which they live, are far from what the Word of God teaches. She examines the Bible, seeking direction for all the areas of her life: how to dress, how to relate to the opposite sex, what to watch on TV, what movie to watch, etc. Sometimes it is difficult and even painful to obey the Lord because the rules of God aren't popular.

She's striving to raise her children to love God and to have a personal relationship with Him. She trusts the Lord as her provider, and knows that He'll give her wisdom to manage her income. For her, her work is a service to God.

Julie suffered a lot when her husband decided to end their marriage, but she recovered with the help of her family and her church. After her divorce, she decided that she and her children would serve the Lord. She wants to be an example of Christian faithfulness to her children. She wants them to remember God´s voice when she prays for them. She wants her children to know that they have a mission in this world for which God has given them life.

Mike

Mike is a 25 year old young man who's been a Christian for a few months and is taking discipleship classes in his church. He's very interested to know Jesus more, which is why he strives to read the Bible and pray every day. He likes going to church because there he learns new things about God. Mike feels that he's in love with his Lord. He deeply admires him and wants to be like him in all areas of his life.

But lately he discovered that it isn't so easy to obey Jesus in everything He asks. Many questions arise in his head: How can we love others as we love ourselves? Is it possible to live without sinning? How can I love and forgive those who've hurt me so much?

Mike wants to get involved in the ministries of the church, and really enjoys serving others. However, sometimes it's difficult for him when there's a program on TV that interests him, or when he wants to stay at home on the weekends to catch up on his sleep.

He admires other Christians who are working in the church, and it seems to him that they have no trouble giving up their free time to be there working alongside the leaders of the ministries. He admires Jessica, for example, a

23-year-old girl who comes to church every Saturday to clean and prepare everything for the Sunday services. He also admires Joseph, an older brother who always greets him with a smile at the door of the sanctuary and knows the name of the more than 100 people who attend! But his favorite is Sonia, who cooks when there's a special event. She was abandoned by her husband many years ago and raised her eight children alone, works as a cashier in a supermarket, and still has time to evangelize and disciple others. She has brought more than five families to church since she became a Christian three years ago!

For Mike, it's difficult to leave the things of his life from before becoming a Christian. He still wants to go out to the nightclubs and dance with his friends. He likes to smoke and occasionally has a cigarette. Mike has discovered that within himself, there's a force that makes it difficult for him to obey God in everything. Sometimes he doubts his salvation because although he wants to be like other Christians, he feels that he'll never become so.

His relationship with his family isn't easy. From time to time he still responds badly to his father. But the biggest problem was with his girlfriend, Paula. She isn't a Christian, and not only doesn't she understand the change that exists in Mike, but she forced him to decide between her and the church. If he wanted to continue with her, he had to prove it to her by starting to live together as a couple (although not married). Mike is in a lot of pain because he loves his girlfriend, but was forced to end the relationship. He trusts that God has a Christian wife for him, and is determined to wait for her.

Mike doesn't want to go back to his old life. He wants with all his heart to have the courage to break with everything in his past that relates to sin. Mike wants to have that inner strength to serve others, and that it wouldn't cost so much to leave other things to devote time to work in the church. Mike knows that the happiness he experiences with Jesus is nothing compared to the happiness that the world gave him, and he wants with all his heart that God would fill him with His love and purity so that he could be more like Jesus.

He wants to be remembered as a courageous man who followed and served Jesus with all his might.

Karen

Karen is aware that there's a God or force of life or higher being, whatever you want to call Him. As a child, her grandmother took her to Sunday School, but she hardly remembers anything from the time there. She has prejudices against the organized church, and distrusts TV evangelists and priests. Sometimes she thinks about God when she's on vacation in the mountains or at sea.

Karen considers herself to be a religious person. For her, God is everywhere. She's recently been curious and started reading books about spiritual life. She's bought biographies of the Dalai Lama, Mahatma Gandhi, Buddha and others. She's tried meditation and psychotherapy to get in touch with her inner being. She believes that within herself, she'll find the key to fulfilling her destiny in this world. For her, the authority of her life is her own enlightened self.

Karen is always in with new trends. In the face of negative opinions on abortion, homosexuality, and euthanasia, she defends the right of each person to choose what they want. She feels that it's the free right of each human being to do what he/she wants to do with their life and body.

Work for her is like a game where each one competes for success, money, power and personal fulfillment. She's determined to succeed in her profession regardless.

She'll get married when she really finds a good candidate. So far, she's thinking of moving in with her current boyfriend to see how it works.

She dreams of having children with a good education and who are successful. She wants her children to remember her as an intelligent, independent, affectionate and fun loving woman.

She wants to be remembered as someone who knows well what she wants, and knows how to fight for her dreams.

Henry

Henry has been a Christian for a long time and knows a lot about God. He can recite Bible verses from memory like no one else, and expresses himself very well in public prayer. Ever since he accepted Jesus as his Savior when he was young, he has prayed at home also.

For him, God is a powerful leader who's busy solving the problems of this world. He doesn't believe that God has an interest in cultivating a personal relationship with him.

Henry prays for the same things over and over again because he thinks that in this way, perhaps by his insistence, God may have mercy and listen to him. Usually his prayers are for things that he himself needs: work, security for his family, etc.

For him, serving God is his responsibility. He's a Christian because he has the right lifestyle, but stops at becoming what he considers to be a fanatic. He likes to share with the people in the church, and to collaborate with the church because it's what God demands of him, and Henry doesn't like to feel guilty.

In addition, he has a network of contacts among the congregation for his work in the Christian radio. He doesn't like it much when the pastor of the church asks for special offerings or asks for his time for some ministry. For him, God is there so that he can enjoy life.

Henry isn't a bad person. He's interested in knowing what God wants for his life, but he usually does what he wants.

For Henry, the Bible is a slightly outdated book on matters of morality and values. Henry lives life according to the norms learned from his parents or his Christian community.

His Christian values are flexible. At home, he watches TV shows and movies that teach values and principles that are in rebellion against the will of God, but he's happy because his children still want to attend the youth group of the church.

For Henry, his work is a way to make a living, and the success he has in his profession is due to his effort and natural talents.

He has high hopes for his family. He strives to give everything to his children. They're teenagers and spend a lot of time with non-Christian friends, but they keep getting good grades at school and aren't as bad or as rude as other neighborhood kids.

Their marriage seems strong, but they have lost the romance after many years of living together. There's a kind of pact between the two of them. As long as he maintains the stable economy of the house, she'll treat him well.

Henry thinks that when they remember him, they'll say, "He and his family tried to serve the Lord." He expects his children to be better Christians than he is, and that they would not hold it against him that he doesn't spend much time with them because of his work.

With whom do you identify?

If it is with Julie, you're satisfied with your current experience with God and you like to grow every day in your relationship with Him.

If it is with Mike, you know God but aren't satisfied with your current relationship and are searching for a deeper experience and relationship.

If it is with Karen, you haven't yet accepted Jesus as Savior and are just living as a religious person.

If it is with Henry, you know God but have opted for a state of spiritual childhood that is extremely dangerous.

RECOMMENDED READINGS:

- Psalms 112
- Psalms 42
- Psalms 1
- Luke 8:4-15
- Revelations 3:14-22

A long and dangerous childhood
Lesson 8

Learning goals:

That the students ...

- Understand that living in the flesh is not a good option for God's sons and daughters.
- Identify if there is evidence in their lives of the dominion of sin over God's will.
- Reflect on the evil that the carnal person causes to himself and the church of the Lord.

Resources

- Have different versions of the Bible.
- Two fruits in season of the same type; one green and the other ripe and sweeter. Good examples could be peaches, pears, papayas, melons, bananas or other fruit where there is a marked difference of flavor when the fruit is ripe. Bring enough for the whole class to have pieces.
- Bring with you a dish or bowl, a knife, toothpicks and serviettes.

Introduction

In the previous lesson, we saw in Henry the life of the carnal believer. He is the typical believer who refuses to grow and go further in his spiritual life. Let's take a look at what we saw about the life of the carnal believer.

What should a Christian do in cases like these? The Bible says that we must restore.

Ask the class to complete Activity 1.

We've set aside this lesson to study this spiritual state of Christians who are living in the flesh, because this is the most serious problem facing the Christian church throughout its history. We may ask ourselves why? What harm can this type of person do? Why don't we let them live the Christian life in their own way? After all, they're like that and don't we have the duty to love them as they are, do we?

If you think this way, you don't have the right information. Carnal Christians have been and are the worst enemies for the advancement of the gospel in this world. To understand it better, look at the comparisons in Activity 2.

Have the students complete Activity 2.

Bible Study

Begin the Bible study by assigning several students to read 1 Corinthians 3:1-4 in different versions of the Bible.

In this chapter of 1 Corinthians, the apostle Paul describes the spiritual situation in which the Christians of Corinth found themselves. He calls them carnal and spiritual babies. He tells them that they're fighting among themselves and that they're like the sinful men and women. This was why the apostle was limited in teaching them deeper spiritual truths, since they were not in a position to understand and put them into practice. It was not that the Corinthians lacked intelligence. They were educated and capable of learning, but they were unable to assimilate the deep truths that God had for their lives.

This state of carnality in which the members of the Corinthian church were living caused problems for the church, for spiritual leaders and for themselves. Let's look at the dangers of the believer remaining indefinitely in this state.

1. An extended childhood

Paul describes the carnal believer as having spent time being a Christian, but who is still a child, a spiritual baby. What does this mean?

In the church, the new believers are normally the spiritual babies. They're learning through discipleship the basic truths of the Word, and are taking their first steps as disciples of Christ. These people, like babies, are very fragile, need a lot of attention and a person to take care of them. In other words, they need to be nurtured very closely. We should always have spiritual babies like these in the church. They indicate that the church is fulfilling its mission of winning the lost for Christ.

But overgrown babies are a different case. Christians who have already been in the church for some time should be more developed. Paul says that these people aren't able to digest or assimilate the spiritual riches that God has prepared for His children. Like children, they can't decide what's best for them. In other words, they're totally incapable of discerning the truth from deception because of their lack of knowledge of divine truths. Paul says that these immature Corinthians hadn't reached the level of spiritual growth expected of them. So, he had to go back to the basics of Christianity with them since there was hardly any difference between them and the non-believers.

Just as a father and a mother worry if their baby doesn't gain weight and doesn't grow in height, Paul was concerned about the Corinthians' lack of growth, which was a symptom of poor spiritual health. These Christians showed the characteristics of spiritual babies. They couldn't help themselves and couldn't help others.

A spiritual baby can't help himself

Carnal Christians don't know how to feed themselves. They depend on their pastors as if they were their mothers. Their pastors are kept busy feeding them, solving relationship problems for them, giving them counsel for any small problem, being asked to intercede for them in prayer, and taking their place carrying out the ministry work they should be doing. Since they have no victory over sin, they return again and again to the sins of their old life. That a Christian, year after year, remains in sin is a sign that something is wrong, just as a child who remains in infancy beyond the time of their normal growth shows signs of illness.

A spiritual baby cannot help others

▌▌▌ Ask a student to read Hebrews 5:11-14. ▌▌▌

Like Paul, the author of the letter to the Hebrews encountered this same difficulty with some Jewish believers who refused to mature. Church leaders couldn't train them to assume responsibilities for ministry in the church. On the contrary, they had to help them because they had no spiritual strength. Because carnal believers can't help themselves, they can't serve as spiritual guides to others.

The author of Hebrews says in 5:12, *"by this time you ought to be teachers…"* These believers had several years of being Christians, but they weren't able to assume responsibilities in the church.

In our time, we often hear pastors complaining about believers who don't take responsibility. At times, we find churches where averages of 100 people attend but they can't fill just the seven places of Sunday School teachers! It's very sad to be in a church where volunteers are needed to do small tasks, such as getting the communion table ready, bringing a plate of food for a shared lunch, or collaborate on an offering for the youth camp of the church, but very few respond. What's happening to us? Why such a lack of interest? Are we like children, incapable of assuming any kind of responsibility? Is it that we lack love and passion for the work of God? All these are symptoms of carnality, and carnality is sin.

In healthy churches, Christians grow. From the moment they accept Christ as Savior, they're constantly discipled until they are ready to assume responsibilities in the Body of Christ. The experience of many of these growing churches around the world shows that it takes an average of two years to prepare a new believer to take on a responsibility to lead others, such as being a discipler or Bible study group leader, or a teacher.

Sometimes we have to acknowledge that it was the fault of local church leaders who have not given priority to discipleship. It's sad when new believers continue to just warm pews each Sunday because there is no concern in their leaders to train them so they can get involved in the service as well.

When the opportunities are given in the local church, and the new believers receive instructions for their level of spiritual development, but there is no progress in their spiritual life and no interest in serving others, the symptoms show carnality.

2. THEY CAN'T RECEIVE THE DEEPER TRUTHS

They "no longer try to understand"

In Hebrews 5:11, we read that these carnal brethren didn't try to understand. It's not that they had any mental or physical impairment that would limit them in learning. They were slow and lazy to hear and assimilate what they were being taught because they rejected the spiritual truths shared with them. What a sad picture! How bad their Christian pastors and teachers must have felt that their teachings fell on deaf ears!

They had not learned

Then in 5:12, the author states that they needed to be taught all over again the first basic truths of the Word of God. These believers were like pupils at school who, having failed the year, had to go back to school and retake the same lessons.

It's important that we understand well what learning is all about. In order for spiritual learning to occur, at least three persons must be involved: the teacher who fulfills the role of educator; the student who fulfills the role of the learner or disciple, and the Holy Spirit who works through the miracle of teaching. It's important to note that if any of these parts don't fulfill its function, then there's no learning. Let's look briefly at the roles of each one.

The teacher is responsible for giving the right food according to the stage of the person's spiritual development. Spiritual babies should be given "milk," or the basic things that are seen in the lessons for new believers. When teachers have more mature students, they can go to the deeper concepts and truths of the Word of God. However, spiritual teaching isn't only the transfer of data and concepts from the teacher to the student. Christian discipleship consists of learning to live like Jesus in all areas of life. So, the teacher or Christian leader is one who teaches how to live, and for that, it's fundamental that they must live as an example. They also need to verify that their students are living according to what is expected of them at each stage of their development.

The student is responsible for taking what he learns and applying it to his daily life. In Christian discipleship, we can't pick and choose what we're going to obey and what we're going to ignore. When we make these kinds of choices, we become carnal. This attitude of the carnal believer can be summed up in the popular saying: "in one ear and out the other." But if the student hears and applies the knowledge of the Word, his life develops normally, and the life of Christ is reflected in his life. He/she grows step by step, receiving more and more of the Holy Spirit.

It's the Holy Spirit who makes it possible for us to understand what we learn through our senses (hearing, sight, touch, etc.). That's to say, it makes sense for our lives. The Spirit also gives us wisdom to put it into practice. However, like all grace that comes from God, it can be resisted. The believer may refuse to make any changes that he knows God asks of him, thereby limiting the Spirit's action in his being.

How do we realize if a person has learned or not? When we can see signs of maturity.

▌▌▌ **Take out the fruit, show them to the class and ask: how do we distinguish mature fruit from under-ripe fruit? Let them express their ideas, while you cut the fruit into pieces and put the pieces into two different plates, one for the mature ones and one for the green bits. Then say ... the best way to know if a fruit is ripe is to try it, right?**

Let them take a piece of fruit from each dish and eat it. Then ask: Which one tastes better? Which do you prefer? What does this teach us? How can we prove that a person is learning and growing in the life of Christ? You can jot down your ideas on the blackboard and then make a synthesis of class opinion in a short sentence. ▌▌▌

They were inexperienced

Then in 5:13, the author states that they lack experience. These people had not experienced many of the things of the Christian life. They had rebelled against putting into practice what they had learned, and for that reason, they weren't growing.

For example, if we learn that we should forgive those who have offended us, and we refuse to do so, we aren't practicing forgiveness. Forgiveness is nothing more than a concept to us, and we won't be able to receive the freedom from that load of hatred or resentment. If we haven't forgiven, then we can't love our enemies. This lack of obedience creates a barrier between our Heavenly Father and the believer, because refusing to obey is a sin.

They weren't able to differentiate the good from evil.

Hebrews 5:14 says, *"But solid food is for the mature, who by constant use have trained themselves to distinguish good from evil."* This statement by the author is saying something which is very important, to which we must pay close attention. The dangerous thing about the life in the flesh is that we finally end up justifying sin, excusing ourselves for doing what doesn't please God.

When the new Christian begins to obey God in small things, obedience in everything else comes naturally, although we know it won't be easy and will require learning discipline. On the other hand, the carnal believer often slips into small things, those that aren't seen, and disobeying God becomes easier, and they fail to develop a hundred percent obedience to the will of God.

This judgment to distinguish the good from evil is only received from the Holy Spirit when

God speaks to us and guides us in our thoughts, to arrive at conclusions about things and situations according to the teaching of the Word of God. Listening to the voice of the Spirit, and letting ourselves be guided by Him, is an exercise that is achieved through practice.

For example, if the Spirit makes me feel bad about the way I responded to a fellow Christian, and I do nothing about it, and instead continue doing it again and again, after a time this voice of the Spirit will be imperceptible to me. Every Christian must develop his inner spiritual senses to hear the inner voice of the Spirit. Not to listen to this voice or ignore it can lead us to live a disoriented life, not knowing how to distinguish between good and bad. This makes it easy for sin to drag us down, and finally to make us go back to a life of sin.

3. SIN AND FAILURE BEGIN TO RULE

The lives of the Corinthians manifested a series of sins, such as jealousy, strife, and dissension (1 Corinthians 3: 3-4). Those believers showed by their behavior and their attitudes that they were continuing to live like people who hadn't been born again. They were carried away by jealousy, envying one another. They divided themselves into groups and argued heatedly to defend their own opinions. Because they couldn't agree, they created divisions between themselves that kept separating them more and more. They didn't do anything to keep the unity because no one was willing to give in.

These believers believed that they were spiritual and mature, but the truth is that it's not possible to be spiritual and divided at the same time. The reason they argued was because of their leadership preferences. Some wanted Paul, others wanted Apollos. Those who claimed to be disciples of Paul didn't want to submit to the leadership of Apollos, and those who claimed to be of Apollos didn't want Paul as their spiritual leader. They were getting carried away by their personal preferences rather than seeking the will of God for their lives and their church.

Sometimes, the tendency of Christians is to overlook these sins that we consider "small," such as jealousy, envy, power struggles and other issues that cause serious damage to fellowship among Christians. Paul here points out the seriousness of the behavior of these Christians, who, having been born again, continued to live and think like those who aren't God's sons and daughters.

Although they considered themselves to be spiritual, their way of thinking and their way of acting showed the opposite. When we give place in our lives to temperamental reactions, pride, envy, divisions, harsh and hurtful words, unforgiving attitudes, speaking badly about someone behind their backs, lack of kindness, lack of interest in helping others, etc., we're showing the fruit of the flesh, and the flesh only produces sin. The flesh is selfish and proud. It doesn't generate kindness. The flesh is the opposite of love, which is the fruit of the Spirit.

··················o **Do ctivity No. 3 of the Activity Worksheet with the group.**

The carnal Christian tries to live like the spiritual Christian, but fails. He strives to be kind, to be humble, to serve, but even if he does at times, he can not bear this fruit permanently in his life. This is because the holy love of God does not flow naturally from his being, and will not do so until the Holy Spirit fills this person completely. Only the Spirit can impart the power to walk in love like Christ.

It is a tragedy when in a church most people are carnal. The whole church becomes selfish, cold, without interest for sinners, they do not care for each other, they look for pleasure, their highest priority is to make money and to obtain material goods, etc. A carnal church is the most effective campaign of Satan to discredit Christ, for these believers deny by their acts the power of Christ to restore the lives of people and bring them to live in love and purity.

4. THE FLESH CAN'T COEXIST WITH SPIRITUAL GIFTS

Spiritual gifts are special abilities given by God to his children when they're saved and adopted into His family. These gifts enable each Christian to contribute to the ministry of the church and serve the world as Christ's followers.

We must not ignore the fact that carnal Christians have also received spiritual gifts. However, we must make a difference between spiritual gifts and the fruit of the Spirit, which is the ability to love God and our fellow men with all our hearts. There were wonderful gifts among the Corinthians, so Paul says, *"I always thank my God for you because of his grace given you in Christ Jesus. For in him you have been enriched in every way—with all kinds of speech and with all knowledge"* (1 Corinthians 1:4-5).

In the second letter, he talks about the many gifts they had, although they liked the spectacular gifts that made them stand out in the group. At the same time, the apostle says that they didn't care in the same way to cultivate the fruit of the Spirit: love, joy, peace, patience, kindness, goodness, faith, meekness and temperance.

Unfortunately in the contemporary church, many carnal Christians come to occupy places of leadership because we live in a world where what is valued is image. Image is what people project of themselves and what people perceive. People often confuse that image with what the person actually is. So when looking for a leader, we usually choose the one who speaks well, sings well, is nice, has a good education, has good presence, is responsible, among other qualities that are visible. All of these things are important, but to choose a spiritual leader, we must look for a person who is not carnal. As we saw in these passages, a carnal believer is not fit to be a spiritual leader of others. Capabilities, good education, and talents can never replace the power of God's holy love.

5. HOW DO WE FIND THE SOLUTION?

⦀ Read together Romans 7:22-25. ⦀

In Romans chapters 5- 8, Paul talks about the human search for a life of true spiritual fellowship with God. The apostle, in order to explain himself better, writes in the first person, that is, he plays the role of a person who goes from natural life to spiritual life.

In this chapter (7), he describes the inner struggle of the carnal believer (the two lions of our previous lesson), and concludes with these words of despair, *"What a wretched man I am! Who will rescue me from this body that is subject to death?"* (7:24). This is the desperate cry of a person who has tried by his own strength to live the life of Christ, but feels miserable, defeated, and at his wits end. This is a painful but necessary experience.

The carnal believer needs to reach rock bottom, for it's the only way he can be fully convinced of the evil of his carnality. Until he is completely sure that there is within him a force of evil that opposes God's will for his life, he won't ask God for help. The Holy Spirit works in our lives to bring us to this point. He makes us see in a mirror how horrible the evil is that is lodged in our being.

Just as the repentant sinner seeks Christ to deliver him from his sin, the believer must come to the certainty of his wickedness and despair so that he may finally come to the point of recognizing that he can never be like Christ in his own strength or by his own intelligence.

In the next lesson, we will see that the only solution to get out of carnality is to completely renounce it. There is no other way to begin to live in the Spirit.

▐▐▌ Encourage students to reflect this week on the suggested Bible readings and to prepare in prayer to make a total and complete surrender of their being to Jesus Christ. ▐▐▌

Definition of key terms

- **Discern:** to distinguish something from another thing, pointing out the difference between them. It commonly refers to being able to distinguish between good and bad.

- **Spiritual gifts:** The ability or abilities received from God through the Holy Spirit to carry out some Christian service; for example teaching, providing for the needs of others, praying for the sick, among others.

- **Fruit of the Spirit:** refers to the results produced by the work of the Holy Spirit in the Christian life and mentioned in Galatians 5:22-23.

Summary

The life of the carnal believer isn't the life God wants for His children. Christ died on the cross to make us totally free from the power of sin. The believer who stubbornly lives in the flesh disobeys God and isn't fit to assume responsibilities of ministry in the church. The Holy Spirit tries to bring the carnal believers to a conviction of the sinful force of evil that inhabits them, to bring them to the point of recognizing that they're powerless to live the life of Christ by their own means, and that only by renouncing the power of sin completely can they receive the fullness of God's Holy Spirit.

Activity Worksheet

What is the life of a carnal believer like? Choose the right option:

a. The relationship with God to the carnal believer is like a ...

__ friend

__ aquaintance

__ husband or wife

b. For the carnal believer, God is ...

__ a powerful and busy leader

__ an affectionate parent

__ a cosmic force

c. Prayers are like ...

__ a shopping list

__ a chat with a friend

__ a desperate plea

d. What he/she likes about the church is:

__ their friends

__ the teaching

__ business contacts

e. They think that life is to...

__ be enjoyed

__ serve others

__ glorify God

f. When looking for guidance, they ...

__ consult God

__ do what they want

__ rely on the Word

g. Their achievements in life are due to ...

__ the provision of God

__ the prayer of a grandmother

__ their natural talents

ACTIVITY 2
In groups of 3-4, examine the following comparisons and then respond to the questions below:

1. If the local church were a football team, carnal Christians would be the ones who score the goals against their own side.
2. If the local church were an operating room, the carnal believers would be those who don't wash their hands.
3. If the local church were a wheat field, the carnal believers would be the weeds that pollute crops.
4. If the local church were an army, carnal believers would be undisciplined soldiers.
5. If the local church were a trucking company, the carnal believers would be those who cause losses to the company's interests.
6. If the local church were a school, the carnal Christians would be the rebellious students.
7. If the local church were a news agency, the carnal believers would be the ones who would deal with the sections of negative news, gossip and promote mundane entertainments.
8. If the local church were a beauty pageant, the carnal believers would not pass the entrance examination.
9. If the local church were a museum of works of art, the carnal believers would be like those paintings where the author's signature can only just be seen.
10. If the local church were a library, carnal believers would be classified as too ordinary.
11. If the local church were a foodstuff enterprise, carnal Christians would not pass quality control.

Do you think some of them are exaggerated? Why?

_____

_____

Can you make a list of good things about carnal Christians? For example, How does a carnal Christian contribute to the spread of the gospel?

_____

_____

_____

_____

Share examples of excuses that Christians use to continue sinning, such as lack of forgiveness, greed, anger, lack of commitment to the work of the church, among others.

_____

_____

_____

ACTIVITY 3

In the column on the left, there is a list of the fruits of love that Paul mentions in 1 Corinthians 13 as the distinctions of the spiritual life. As we saw, life in the flesh is the opposite of life in the Spirit. These are included in the list on the right. Mark on both lists which are the most frequent behaviors in your life these days.

	Evidence of spiritual maturity		Evidence of carnal immaturity
	Patient in everything.		Impatient
	Always kind, attentive, affectionate.		Rude, treats people badly
	Not envious.		Envious
	Doesn't believe he/she is more important than others		Haughty, vain
	Humble		Proud
	Kind, polite, respectful.		Bad mannered, impolite, disrespectful
	Generous.		Selfish, always putting themselves first
	Doesn't easily get angry about anything.		Gets angry easily.
	Forgives and forgets offenses.		Spends life remembering how badly others have treated him/her
	Applauds those who speak truthfully.		Applauds evil doers.
	Expects the best of people and God.		Doesn't trust people or God.

If you have most of the marks in the second column, you need to be free from the mastery of the flesh in your life. If you have just a few, you also need to grow in those specific areas.

RECOMMENDED READINGS

- Acts 5:1-11
- Philippians 3
- 1 John 2: 7-17
- Galatians 5
- Galatians 6

How to receive the fullness of the Spirit of love
Lesson 9

Learning goals:

That the students ...

- Know the life of holy love which God wants us to lead.
- Understand that only by giving up self-government and self-idolatry can we be filled with the Holy Spirit.
- Be encouraged to pray to be filled with the Holy Spirit.

Resources

- Two ballpoint pens or other gifts to give to the winners
- A very large transparent jar, a large stone and other smaller stones of different sizes and some sand.
- Practice this demonstration before doing it in class. Put the big stone first in the jar, and then put in the other stones, from the largest to the smallest ones, until you fill the jar. Then add sand along the edges. This is because in the class, you'll take the jar filled with these elements, empty it and ask the students to re-insert all the elements. It's important not to tell them the secret of putting in the big stones first and let them try for a time to see if they can achieve the goal of putting in all the elements.

Introduction

Begin the class by showing the full jar and tell them the following: the spirit-filled believer's life closely resembles this jar. God wants to fill us to the brim with His Spirit, completely full of His love and purity. But for God to fill us, we have to empty ourselves first (empty the contents of the jar on a tray). In this class, we'll talk about how this process of being filled with the Holy Spirit happens, and for this I'll ask two volunteers to put all these items back into the jar.

Put the volunteers in a visible place so that the students can see them while they work. The instructions are to put everything in the jar in 1 minute. They have one chance and there should be nothing left. If they succeed, they get the prize.

However, they're likely to fail. Thank the volunteers and point to the jar as you ask the class: why couldn't they put all the items into the jar?

Listen to the answers and then say: do you think you could have done it if you had been shown how to do it? Let's see what the secret is as we study in the Word what it says we must do so that God can fill us completely with his Spirit and give us all those blessings he's reserved for us.

If they do fill the jar by putting the big stones first, congratulate them and give them the prizes. Then say that they did the right thing - they put the biggest most important stones in first.

As we'll see in this lesson, to be filled with the Holy Spirit, we must give God the place of importance that He deserves in our lives.

Bible Study

1. Do you wish with all your heart to be holy as God is holy?

The first step in preparing our lives is to be sure that we want this experience. What is this experience? The Scriptures speak of holiness in many different ways. For example, holiness is described as:

- A complete surrender of our whole being to God (consecration).
- To be sanctified, that is, trained by God to live in purity.
- Be filled with the Spirit.

- The second work of grace.
- To be made perfect in love.
- Christian perfection.
- The baptism of the Holy Spirit.
- Entire sanctification.
- Dying to self.
- A pure life and heart.
- To be like Christ.
- Live in purity like Christ.
- To be restored to the image of Christ.

Ask the students to complete Activity 1.

All these ways of describing holiness may confuse us, but in reality, God's purpose is to show us in many ways the same truth so that we may understand it better. There are two aspects that are central to the life of holiness that will help us understand this experience better.

God fills us with his holy love

What does God fill us with? When the Bible says that God fills us with his holiness, what He means is that He gives us of his own nature, and the nature of God is love.

When God fills us with his Holy Spirit, He fills us with love. But it's not some kind of love that human beings have practiced. This love is the same love that unites the three persons of the Holy Trinity. It's the love with which the Father loves the Son, the love of the Son for the Father and the Spirit, and the love of the Spirit for the Father and the Son. That's why we can safely say that the life of God is love. God lives to love and can't do anything but love. Everything He's done, all His decisions, all His laws, are deeply rooted in His love.

God saves us to fill us with this divine love, and then offers to lead us by the hand to learn to live this life of love, full of His love.

⫻ Have a student read 2 Peter 1:4 out loud. ⫻

Then ask the class to complete Activity 2.

⫻ Let them share freely. What is the life of holiness? ⫻

God has promised to enable us to love God and our fellow human beings perfectly. In this way, every Christian has the privilege that only a son or daughter of God can have of being a partaker of the divine nature. When God fills us with His love, He fills us with His very essence.

When we're filled with the Spirit, there's no place for sin. Love for God urges us to love what

He loves and to hate what He hates. The result is a life of purity, delivered from everything worldly to serve God with our lives.

Tell the class to complete Activity 3. It includes a test so that they can evaluate if they really want this experience with their whole being.

2. WE MUST EMPTY OURSELVES.

Secondly, we must be willing to surrender our lives totally and forever to Jesus Christ. To be filled with the Spirit, we must empty ourselves first.

||| Empty the jar as you speak. |||

When we're saved, the Holy Spirit comes to live in our lives, but God's love can't fill us completely because within us there still remains selfish love. This selfish love is the sin inherited by the entire race from our first parents. This love drives us to love the world and sin, leads us to put our will above all others, and to love ourselves above all others, including God.

John Wesley taught that no Christian is ready to be filled with the perfect love of God until he's free from all sin inside and out. Until sin is cast out, the love of God can't occupy the full capacity of the soul.

How can you empty yourself in this way? There are three very important steps that must be taken before someone can be filled by God with His holy love.

Resign self-government

When we begin the Christian life, we accept Christ as our Lord and Savior. To recognize that Christ is our Lord by the will of the Father is one thing, but to make the changes in our lives so that Christ can really be king is another.

If we want to be filled with the Holy Spirit, we must be willing to live in the Kingdom of God. The Kingdom of God isn't like our democratic governments in which we elect our rulers, and then we may or may not agree with them, or we may even vote against them in the next election.

In the Christian life, there's only one form of government that God has established, and it's a theocracy. In it, God is the absolute sovereign to whom his servants obey through love. This king rules in love, and the people choose to be in his kingdom by their own choice. His subjects live their lives according to the will of God, not out of fear of punishment, but because they are convinced that His will is perfect for their lives.

We shouldn't be afraid of failing to live the life of purity that Jesus lived, for none of us will achieve that through our personal effort. That's why we have to give up control of our lives and abandon ourselves completely to God. When the Holy Spirit fills our life, He enables us to love God and love His will. So God not only asks us to live like Jesus in perfect obedience to His will, but He also gives us the "power" of love that enables us to do so.

Self-government is when someone takes control of their own life. When this happens, they can't love God and others with all their heart.

Give up self-idolatry

Idolatry is surrendering oneself to something, giving it the honor and place that only our Creator deserves. It can be an angel, an image, a family member, a vice, a sport, a religion ... and above all ... oneself.

Self-worship is putting oneself in first place, rather than giving it to God. We were born with the sinful tendency to love ourselves above all else. God deserves to have first place in our lives. He deserves to be our first and great love; the one who's above anything or anyone else.

Our self-will within us will always try to lead us to do what we want, and we're used to listening to its voice. It must be removed from the place of importance that it's always had. It needs to be made humble and learn to obey the Holy Spirit.

We have to die

||| Ask a volunteer to read Mark 8:34. |||

When Jesus asks us as His disciples to deny ourselves and take up our cross, He's asking us to give up our willful nature. This is the least we can do for Him, for all He did for us when He gave His life on the cross to die for our sins.

||| Read Philippians 2:5-8 and ask, what did Christ do for our sake? |||

Taking up the cross means to renounce our own life, to die to oneself, renouncing self-government and renouncing self-idolatry. When we do this, we renounce everything that opposes God, like wrong thinking, bad attitudes and bad desires. The apostles could be filled with the Spirit because they were willing to die to themselves. Let's see the testimony of Paul.

||| Have another student read Galatians 2:20. |||

The only way to live the life of Christ is to allow Him to live in us. We must stop leaning on our pride, our abilities, our experience, and our name, and surrender completely to the direction of God, just as a blind man is guided by his guide dog.

When God fills us with His Spirit of love, then Christ becomes part of our lives. At the moment of surrender, we make a covenant with God, and He signs it by filling us with His Spirit. We no longer govern ourselves alone, but our spirit dialogs with the Spirit and we decide what is best for our life, for our church, for our family. The one who directs and advises us is the Spirit of love, and the love of God is never wrong.

3. GIVING OURSELVES TOTALLY TO GOD

....o **Start this section by doing Activity 4.**

||| Have another volunteer read Romans 12:1-2. |||

In this passage, the Apostle Paul begs the brothers of the church in Rome to make this surrender of their whole being to the Lord, presenting their bodies as a living sacrifice, holy and pleasing to

God. Let's see what Paul's message adds to our understanding of the surrender that God requires of us..

Presenting ourselves as a living sacrifice

In antiquity, many religious rituals included making sacrifices. These consisted of giving to the gods an animal or some other type of offering which was burned on an altar. In the case of the people of Israel, they used to give offerings to God to show their gratitude for something God gave them, or as a sign of repentance. God himself established these sacrifices for the people of Israel so that when Jesus Christ came, they might recognize him as the perfect lamb that takes away the sin of the world (John 1:29). These animal sacrifices consisted of delivering the living animal to the priest to kill by cutting the jugular vein so that the animal would bleed. They would then burn the body on the temple altar.

But there is a great difference in that sacrifice and the one that Paul is speaking about. It's not a matter of delivering a dead body, but of giving ourselves up as a living offering to continue living for God.

This is not a sacrifice to obtain forgiveness from God, but a sacrifice of praise. We give our life to God so that He can form in us the life of Christ, and thus glorify himself, showing his love to the world.

Not conforming to the pattern of this world

The children of God don't belong to this world; we belong to the kingdom of God. This kingdom is present in the heart of each of His children. However, the Christian's temptation is to adapt to the sins that dominate the people in our context. This is a custom that many Christians have, and even the leaders of many churches adapt their lives and twist the Word of God so that they have an excuse to live in the sinful way of the world.

For many Christians, the line between good and bad is blurred. If you ask them, what do you think about abortion? What does the Bible say about homosexuality? Maybe we can tell a lie sometimes? Is it okay to let our anger burst out, hurting others with our words? You will not always get a satisfactory answer.

The way of life of people who are non-Christians doesn't represent a model for the Christian who wants to live the life of Christ.

To be transformed by the renewing of the mind.

This word used by Paul to describe the change that the Spirit produces in the lives of the sons and daughters of God is "metamorphosis." It's the same word used in Matthew 17:2 to describe the transfiguration of Christ (also in Mark 9:2). This is a word that's used a lot in science to describe the total and complete change that's a part of the growth process of many living creatures. For example, the caterpillar weaves a cocoon where it will be enclosed for a time, and then it will continue its existence as a butterfly.

What the apostle says here is that the Spirit brings to the believer's life a radical change in thinking. This is a 180 degree turn by which we desire to have the mind of Christ and give the Holy Spirit access and permission to transform us step by step, day by day. This will make us more and more like our Lord. Changing the way we think is essential to changing the way we feel and live.

4. THE FULLNESS OF THE HOLY SPIRIT IS RECEIVED BY FAITH

The fullness of the Spirit is received by faith, just as we receive salvation. There are Christians who spend days fasting and praying, thinking that in this way, they will convince God that they deserve to be filled with His Spirit. Fasting and praying aren't bad, but the fundamental purpose of these disciplines should be to subdue our will and examine ourselves to be prepared for this experience. God doesn't expect us to beg Him to fill us with His Spirit. He wants to do it and is ready to fill us with His Love whenever we ask Him!

Let's look at this comparison. If you write a check from your bank account and want to get cash for it, what do you do? Do you go to the bank teller and get down on your knees begging him to give you the money? No, because it's not necessary. You have money in that bank and know that when you need it, they'll give it to you. This experience is like a check we can collect at any time. God has a bank full of spiritual riches, and they are there for us to make them effective in our lives!

Some Christians spend a lot of time waiting for this experience of the Spirit because they are confused. They're looking for some emotional manifestation, a sign or an angel that comes down from heaven and to tell them that it has been done. But this won't happen, because the fullness of the love of God is received by faith. It's as simple as when we were saved. In the same way that God called us to salvation, He calls us now to be filled with the Spirit.

[[[Have a student read 1 Peter 1:2-5.]]]

The apostle Peter says that we are *"chosen according to the foreknowledge of God the Father,"* which means that God's will from the time he saved us is that we should be fully sanctified. In His wisdom, God has drawn up a perfect plan to completely restore us from sin and lead us to live in the purity of love. Then he says that *"he has given us new birth into a living hope."* This means that through the sacrifice of Christ on the cross, God has given us a new life so that we may begin to live it on this earth, free from the corruption of sin. For the Christian, eternal life begins when we receive Christ as Savior.

Both salvation and the fullness of the Spirit, and the life of growth that comes next, is the path God has chosen and designed for each of his sons and daughters. So there's no doubt that God wants to fill us with His Spirit. What we must make sure we do first is to prepare our heart so that it can be filled.

[[[Take the empty jar now and say: "in order that God may fill us completely with His Spirit of love, we must follow the right order. First we must empty our life and renounce all the forms of sin that have led us to a life of self-government and self-idolatry."

Put the big stone in first and say: "the first thing God is going to give us is his Holy Spirit. This will occupy the main place in our life."

Put in the other stones - from the biggest to the smallest - and say: "The Holy Spirit brings with it the perfect love of God that will fill our lives with good intentions, good thoughts, good attitudes and good works ... making all the changes that are necessary to reproduce in us the life of Christ."

Then finally add the sand until the jar is full to the top and say: "this love of God will give wonderful fruits and countless blessings, just as the grains of sand are filling up all the spaces. By means of these fruits, people will be able to see and experience the love of Christ. We won't be able to count them because giving love will be the natural thing

that springs from our life. The important thing is not to count the grains of sand, but to see how beautifully it's spread on the beach providing rest to those who are tired." ▌▌▌

▌▌▌ Ask a student to read John 7:37-39 and ask the class. "What is the living water that Jesus promised to give to everyone who asks for it?"

Finish filling up the jar with water and say: "The Holy Spirit is the water of life promised by Jesus to each of his sons and daughters. Until you're filled completely with Him, you won't be able to experience what it is to be truly alive. To be alive for God is to be completely free from sin in order to love as God loves us, and this can only be done when the Spirit completely fills us.

Do you want to have this life of God spilling out of your being to everyone around you? Do you want to be filled with the Spirit of Love right now?" ▌▌▌

o In Activity 5, there is a guide included so that you can lead the students to pray to ask God to fill them with his Spirit of Love. If there isn't any time in the class, encourage the students to take a special time during the week and say this prayer, asking God to fill them with his Holy Spirit.

Definition of key terms

- **Consecration:** an act of dedicating something to the service of God exclusively. It can be a person's life, his time, goods and even others.

- **Holy, pure:** a holy or pure Christian is one who has been filled with the Holy Spirit and as a result is living a life close to God and away from sin.

- **Sanctified:** a person who has been filled with the Holy Spirit

- **Second work of grace:** after the first work of grace, which we know as Salvation, will follow another experience called "second work of grace" or "entire sanctification". Entire sanctification is the grace received from God when the believer receives by faith the fullness of the Holy Spirit, which enables him to live a life of holiness.

- **The baptism of the Holy Spirit:** the second work of the Holy Spirit in the human heart, a time after conversion, which results in purity of heart and power for service. It occurs when a person reaches the point of total consecration or surrender to God. This baptism is what happened to the disciples of Christ on the day of Pentecost.

- **John Wesley:** an Anglican minister of the eighteenth century, founder of Methodism, who rediscovered in the Bible that the will of God for his children is to live a life of love and purity, filled with the Holy Spirit. Those churches that follow Wesley, such as the Church of the Nazarene, are called Holiness Churches.

Summary

God's will for the lives of His sons and daughters is that they can love in the same way that He loves them, without any kind of selfish interest. This perfect love unites the three persons of the Holy Trinity. It's this love that led the Father to give his only Son, Jesus Christ, for our salvation. If we don't possess the love of God, we can't serve this world as Christ did.

For God to fill us with His love, we must first give up the selfishness that resides in our inner being and fights against God's will for our lives. This sin doesn't allow God to really be the king of our life, and prevents us from loving God with our whole being. In order to be filled with the Spirit of love, we must die to ourselves.

The fullness of the Spirit is received with a prayer of faith. From then on, through a continuous relationship with God, He'll transform and teach us to live and love like Jesus.

Activity Worksheet

ACTIVITY 1

In the following ways in which the holy life is described in the Bible, which have you not heard of so far or you are not sure what they mean? Mark them an X. Then at the end of the class if you still have questions about any of them you can ask for more explanation from your teacher.

___ A complete surrender of our whole being to God or consecration.

___ Being sanctified, that is, trained by God to live in purity.

___ Being filled with the Spirit.

___ The second work of grace.

___ Being made perfect in love.

___ Christian perfection.

___ The baptism of the Holy Spirit.

___ Entire sanctification.

___ Dying to self.

___ Purity of life and heart.

___ To be like Christ.

___ To live in purity like Christ.

___ To be restored to the image of Christ.

ACTIVITY 2.

What does it mean to live in holiness according to 2 Peter 1:3-4?

"His divine power has given us everything we need for a godly life through our knowledge of him who called us by his own glory and goodness. Through these he has given us his very great and precious promises, so that through them you may participate in the divine nature, having escaped the corruption in the world caused by evil desires."

_____

_____

_____

_____

_____

ACTIVITY 3.

Do you want with all your heart to be filled with the Spirit of love? Answer the following questions with yes or no.

___ Are you tired of struggling in the Christian life with your own strength?

___ Are you often weak to control negative thoughts that make you think badly about your christian brothers and sisters and and your leaders?

___ Do you have a hard time to stop talking about others, and then regretting it?

___ Would you like to have more faith and trust in God?

___ Would you like to pray with more conviction that God will respond to your prayers?

___ Are you tired of doing things in your own strength instead of having patience to wait for God to do them?

___ Do you feel bad when you often show pride in your abilities and believe you are better than others?

___ Would you like to love others as they are instead of always looking for their faults?

___ Do you have difficulty putting God first in your life, thinking that you know what is best?

___ Would you like to have no trouble giving tithes and offerings?

___ Would you like to have no problem giving your time to the ministry of the church?

___ Are you tired of the fight inside you rebelling against what you know is right?

___ Would you like to be better known for your kindness than for your bad moods?

___ Do you often have mood swings that lead you to be inconsistent in your spiritual life?

___ Would you like to know more about Jesus and enjoy his fellowship?

___ Would you like your life to be an instrument of blessing in the lives of other people?

___ Do you want your life to be clean of all selfishness that separates you from God?

If most of your answers are yes, then do not delay in asking God to fill you with His Spirit.

ACTIVITY 4.

Read this selected piece from author Keith Drury's book "Holiness for All Believers" and then answer the questions below.

"Most Christians sooner or later realize one or both of these problems: 1. an inner inclination to disobey the Lord, which may result in sinning, especially in committing sins of attitude or thinking; 2. a lack of power and motivation to do God's work in the world because of being lukewarm, indifference and coldness of heart."

A.   What do you think of what this author says? Have you had any problems like these in your life?

_____

_____

B.   For this author the problem is that God is not completely Lord of the life of the Christian, or that this has decided to be his own boss. Do you agree?

_____

_____

C. What do you think is the solution to these problems? What do these Christians lack?

_____

_____

ACTIVITY 5.
Pray to ask God to fill you with His Spirit of Love

Your prayer can follow the following order:

1. Tell God how much you want to be filled with His Spirit and why.

2. Give up self-government and self-idolatry and ask God to cleanse you from the sinful desires of the flesh that are opposed to His will for your life.

3. Confess all sin that the Holy Spirit brings to your mind, for example: if you have offended someone, if you have not been faithful to God in something, etc.

4. Give all your life to the Lord, including your past, your present and your future. Include your abilities.

5. Ask the Lord to fill you with His Holy Spirit and flood your life with His love, and receive it by faith.

6. Thank God for filling your life with His Spirit.

RECOMMENDED READINGS

- Philippians 1: 1:11
- Philippians 1: 12-30
- Philippians 2: 1-30
- Philippians 3
- Philippians 4

From Simon to Peter: Internal changes resulting from the fullness of the Spirit
Lesson 10

Learning goals:

That the students ...

- Know the inner work that the Holy Spirit has done in their lives when they were filled with the love of God.
- Understand that the fullness of the Spirit is the beginning of a life free from the dominion of sin.
- Make a commitment to persevere in this experience of purity, reaffirming their commitment to God every day.

Resources

- Bring to the class two or three devices that require batteries to operate, such as a radio or music player, a flashlight, an alarm clock, or others.

Introduction

Begin the class by asking students to share experiences they had during the week in prayer to receive the fullness of the Spirit of love.

In this lesson, we'll talk about the internal changes that occur in the lives of Christians when God fills them with His Spirit of love.

Have a student read Matthew 14:22-33. Then write on the board: "From Simon to Peter."

One of the most astounding changes in the life of a Christian when receiving the fullness of the Holy Spirit that the Bible tells us about is that of Simon Peter.

John and Andrew were the first disciples to be called by Jesus. Andrew was Simon's brother, and that same day he went and sought out his brother. John was James's brother and did the same thing as Andrew, taking his brother to Jesus. This group of brothers had known each other since they were children. They were from the same city and shared a fishing company. Simon was the leader of this team of fishermen.

What was Simon like? Simon was anxious and ambitious. He was bold, sincere and determined. He often excelled in initiative. While the other disciples were still pondering a question, Simon was giving his answer.

Simon liked being in the center of the action. That is why, in the midst of the storm, as Matthew narrates, while the other disciples are clinging to the sides of the boat, Simon takes a walk on the water without thinking twice. We must recognize that Simon was brave. We must not forget that when Simon sank, he had already walked on the water of the lake! In other words, he had the courage to go out there, which the others didn't have. He also followed Jesus to the court of the High Priest with John. The others had fled, but he remained there until the cock crowed.

Simon liked to talk, talk and talk. He was curious and asked questions. In the Gospels, he asks more questions than all the other apostles together, and if we look at the first chapters of Acts - where John and Simon are inseparable - Simon is the one who always speaks, while John prefers to say nothing.

Obviously, Simon wasn't perfect. One of his weaknesses was the habit of speaking without thinking. Simon was impetuous, inconsistent, untrustworthy, and made big promises that he couldn't keep. He was one of those people who got into an ambitious project but gave up before finishing it. He was the first to enter and the first to leave. He was the typical double-minded carnal person, and he fit in very well with what James says, "Such a person is double-minded and unstable in all they do" (1:8).

How was the life of this man transformed in his walk as one of Jesus' disciples?

Bible Study

1. JESUS CHANGED HIS NAME.

The name Simon was a common name. In the Gospels, at least seven different people named Simon are mentioned.

- Simon the Zealot was another of the 12 (Matthew 10:4).
- One of Jesus' brothers (Matthew 13:55).
- The father of Judas Iscariot (John 6:1).
- Simon the leper - Jesus ate at his house (Matthew 26:6).
- A Pharisee where Jesus ate (Luke 7:36-40).
- The one who carried the cross - Simon of Cyrene (Matthew 27:32).

His full name was Simon the son of Jonah or "John" (which is sometimes translated Jonah) (Matthew 16:17; John 21:15-17). Except for the name of his parents, and that his brother was called Andrew, we don't know anything else about his family.

▌▌ Ask a student to read John 1:42. Here the Bible narrates Simon's first encounter with Jesus: "Jesus looked at him and said, 'You are Simon, son of John. You will be called Cephas' (which, when translated, is Peter)." Peter was a kind of nickname that means "rock" or "a piece of rock" ("Petros" in Greek and "Cephas" in Aramaic). ▌▌

Jesus had a purpose in changing his name.

It seems that Jesus changed Peter's name so that Peter would always remember what he was to become. This impetuous, aggressive and impatient Simon had to become Peter, a rock, in the hands of Jesus.

···○   Ask the students to complete Activity 1.

Like these examples, Simon needed to believe that Jesus was going to turn him into a rock, that is, someone who can be believed in, someone others could follow.

Jesus sometimes calls him Simon and sometimes Peter

One very interesting aspect of Jesus as Master is to see the way he dealt with Simon. Jesus not only gave him a new name, but - from then on - sometimes he called him Simon and sometimes Peter. Every time Peter does something that needs to be corrected, he calls him by his old name, Simon. We will see some of these cases in the next point.

2. THE OLD SIMON KEEPS ON REAPPEARING.

Simon the "know-it-all"

Luke 5:5 says, "Simon answered, 'Master, we've worked hard all night and haven't caught anything. But because you say so, I will let down the nets.' Who spoke here? It was the old fisherman Simon who doesn't believe that Jesus is right. He probably was saying to himself something like: "How could Jesus know about this? He has never been a fisherman?"

On this occasion, Simon demonstrates very little desire to obey Jesus. Perhaps he said to himself: "Does the Master not know how tired we are and how frustrated we feel? Do you think we slept all night? Do you doubt that we've really done our best, that we've tried everything without any result?"

However, we then see in verse 8 that Simon recognizes that Jesus is the Lord, and therefore knows more than him and has control over all nature. Luke describes this scene by saying, "When Simon Peter saw this, he fell at Jesus' knees and said, 'Go away from me, Lord; I am a sinful man!'"

The Holy Spirit was allowing the old carnal nature to surface in Simon so that he could realize that there was a sinful tendency in his life – a tendency that needed to be cleansed so that he could be the Peter that Jesus wanted him to be.

Simon the undisciplined

Luke relates one of the most serious failures that Pedro had to face in his career as a disciple: He betrayed his teacher. Jesus had warned Peter that this was going to happen, as we read in Luke 22:31, *"Simon, Simon, Satan has asked to sift all of you as wheat."*

In the garden of Gethsemane, Peter couldn't keep praying as Jesus had asked, and fell asleep. Mark writes, *"Then he returned to his disciples and found them sleeping. 'Simon,' he said to Peter, 'are you asleep? Couldn't you keep watch for one hour? Watch and pray so that you will not fall into temptation. The spirit is willing, but the flesh is weak.' "* (Mark 14:37-38).

Every time Jesus called him Simon, Peter wasn't doing so well. Inside, he wanted Jesus to call him Rock. But Jesus only called him a Rock when he thought, spoke and acted correctly.

Simon the impatient

The last time Jesus calls him Simon was after his resurrection.

||| Assign a student to read: John 21:3 and John 21:15-19. |||

Jesus had asked them to go to Galilee where He would meet them. However, Simon grew tired of waiting and went to Galilea to fish in the lake, accompanied by the other disciples. They fished all night and didn't get anything. In the morning, they were exhausted, and in the distance, they see Jesus on the beach waiting for them with a tasty breakfast.

After eating together, Jesus talks to Peter about his betrayal in the courtyard of the High Priest while he was subjected to questioning. Simon was probably trying to avoid this confrontation. He had denied knowing Jesus or being his friend three times, even though he had promised before the whole group of disciples that he would follow Christ, even to his death.

Jesus understood the human nature that was fighting inside Peter. Peter was like many of us; sometimes he acted in his fleshly nature or in the customs of his life before being a Christian, and at other times he behaved like a true child of God.

The Gospel of John says that Jesus asked him the same question three times: *"Simon son of Jonah, do you love me?" And three times Peter answered, "Yes Lord, you know that I love you ..."* What did Jesus ask him to do to prove his love? He needed to become a shepherd for other believers, both for the spiritual babies (lambs) as well as for the already mature (sheep). In order to be able to care for and guide people in the Christian life, Simon had to be turned into Peter. That was the last time Jesus called him Simon.

The main task for which God enables us when he fills us with his Spirit is to make disciples, that is, to care for others in their spiritual development and to teach them to live the life of Christ. For this, much patience is necessary, and patience is one of the fruit of the Spirit.

It was in this last encounter with Jesus that Simon finally understood that in order to serve his Lord, he had to let Jesus Christ transform him with the power of His Spirit.

3. Results of the Spirit's Filling

||| Assign two students to read Acts 1:8 and 2:1-7. |||

It took Jesus three and a half years of discipling Peter, but at last Peter understood that he couldn't live the life of Christ in his own strength. As we see in Acts 1:8, Peter obeyed his Lord and waited for the promise of the Holy Spirit. On the day of Pentecost, a few weeks after his last encounter with Jesus, Simon was filled with the Spirit and his life was transformed.

This was the first time in history that the Holy Spirit came to stay in the hearts of the children of God. Jesus had been filled with the Spirit, and this was possible because there was no sin in his life. On the other hand, for the Spirit to come to live in the hearts of the disciples, something had to happen first - the death and resurrection of Jesus Christ. Only then could sin be cleansed from their hearts.

As Hebrews 13:12 says, *"And so Jesus also suffered outside the city gate to make the people holy through his own blood."* The changes in Peter's life are evident. He was the one who stood up and boldly preached a tremendous sermon, and three thousand people were converted. Peter never turned back. Filled with the Holy Spirit, Peter was ready to serve his Lord. How did this happen? This was possible because someone loved Peter so much that he invested his life so that he could be transformed.

Jesus promised His disciples that the fullness of the Spirit would bring power to their lives. Let's look at some of the obvious changes that this power of the Spirit of God brought to the life of Peter.

The Holy Spirit empowers the believer's life

The Greek word that is translated "power' is "dunamis" that comes from the verb "dunamai" which means "to be able." When Jesus promises the Spirit of power, He is telling them that He will send them an enabling force so they can undertake the spreading of the gospel in the world.

||| Show the electrical appliances and ask the class some questions like these, while you do the demonstration: Why were these apparatuses made? From where do they get their power, or energy to function and fulfill their purpose? Do they work

if they are close to the source of power? (While saying this approach the batteries). Where should the power source be installed to work? Do they have any use if they are disconnected from the power source? What does this illustration teach us about the Christian life?

The only source of power for the Christian is the Holy Spirit. The Holy Spirit empowers believers with a supernatural power that infuses them with purity, power, courage and spiritual energy to be witnesses, and to pray, have perfect love and an abundance of spiritual fruit and peace. All these requirements are necessary to carry out the mission entrusted to us by the Lord, enabling us to make disciples for Jesus in all nations. Let's briefly see in this lesson the power to live in purity, to witness, and to pray, which are evident in the experience and teachings of the apostle Peter. We'll study the other results of the fullness of the Spirit in the next lesson.

Power to live a holy life

1 Peter 1:15-16 says that God's call to his children is to be holy as He is holy. The power of the Spirit fills our heart with the holy love of God, and this enables us to grow in love. This love residing within us identifies us with the God of holy love. If we love God with our whole being, we'll do everything possible to please Him. We'll no longer wish to return to sin or do anything that offends or brings shame to our Father. It's this power of love that enables us to obey God.

The Spirit-filled life doesn't prevent us from sinning again, but the life of the sanctified believer is one of continual cleansing. The Holy Spirit acts in us as a traffic light guiding us to do what God wants, bringing us peace. When we are doing what God wants, the light is green. When we are in danger of doing something sinful, the yellow warning light comes on to prevent us from doing something outside of God´s will. The red light tells us that we have done something wrong and we must stop and repair the damage.

Spirit-filled Christians perceive this inner power, the love of God, which is like a river continuing flowing and showing itself in their lives.

Ask the students to do Activity 2.

Power for effective testimony and service

In Matthew 28:18-20, we read that the call to make disciples is for all believers. However, Peter's cowardice kept him from fulfilling this command. Like many of us, Peter was afraid of a task that was unpopular. Only when he was filled with the Spirit was it easy for him to fulfill God's purpose for his life. Even in the face of the threat of persecution, he remained in Jerusalem and kept preaching the gospel.

The Spirit of love empowers us with a special compassion for people who suffer because of sin. Being a witness of Christ is not an option for the Spirit-filled believer. The greatest and most powerful force of love that exists in the universe is in your heart, and it drives you to do something so that people can know Christ. As we see in the example of Stephen, this passion cannot be quenched even by trials and martyrdom (Acts 7: 55-60). All Christians can testify that there's a big difference when we testify full of the power of the Spirit.

Ask the students to complete Activity 3.

Power of prayer

Ask a student to read 1 Peter 2:5, 9.

One of the priest's responsibilities in Israel was to pray intercessory prayers for the people. God's plan since the coming of Christ is that all Christians should be priests, and that we can turn to God with all confidence.

Any Christian can pray, but the prayer of the Spirit-filled believer is different.

Ask a student to read Romans 8:26.

This verse says that the Spirit helps us. The believer and the Spirit are two people who turn to God together. The Holy Spirit stands by us and supplies us with what we humanly lack to pray as necessary. Sometimes when we cannot find the words to express our emotions to God, or when we don't know what to ask for, it's best to be quiet and silent in pouring out our lives in the presence of God. We can have the confidence that the Spirit will bring our petition before God. The Spirit stands in solidarity with God's sons and daughters, and cries out for us. It's wonderful to have this permanent help in our lives.

Ask the class to complete Activity 4.

4. PAST AND PRESENT IN THE SERVICE OF THE LORD

Peter continued to use both names for himself. In his letters he signs:

"Simon Peter, servant and apostle of Jesus Christ" (1 Peter 1:1). He took the nickname Jesus gave him as his last name. The surname is the one that indicates our ancestry, our lineage, and our family. Peter says in 1 Peter 2:9-10, *"But you are a chosen people, a royal priesthood, a holy nation, God's special possession, that you may declare the praises of him who called you out of darkness into his wonderful light. Once you were not a people, but now you are the people of God; once you had not received mercy, but now you have received mercy."*

Simon now had the inner assurance that he was part of the family of Christ. He was filled with the Holy Spirit, and he allowed Jesus to be the Lord of all his life and ministry. It's wonderful to know that the Holy Spirit doesn't eliminate our past. He doesn't subject us to brainwashing. On the contrary, being filled with the Holy Spirit can help us be at peace with ourselves, accept our history, accept ourselves as we are, recognize our defects and appreciate our virtues. In other words, we learn to see ourselves, to value ourselves and to love ourselves as God loves us! Not thinking that we are better or that we are have less worth than others, but having a more balanced and true vision of who we are.

It is beautiful to know that God doesn't reject our past. Our past is part of who we are, but He makes our history a powerful tool for influencing the lives of other people. If sin has left its marks, these marks become a living testimony of the restorative work that Jesus Christ has done in us. If we have valuable gifts, God sees them as a treasure that earns interest continuously because it will be invested in the transformation of the lives of our fellow man.

||| Ask a student to read 1 Peter 2:4-10. |||

All people, even Christians, are looking for a firm rock in which to anchor the boat of their life. Life in this world is a sea full of merciless storms. These storms shake us, hurt us, and fill us with fear. We humans seek to secure our lives to many things, such as in the case of Peter, to ourselves, for others it will be to material goods, to their spouse or friends, to a spiritual leader, to their knowledge, etc. …

However, to be filled with the Spirit, Peter had to hit rock bottom and realize that the only sure Rock to anchor life is Jesus Christ. In this passage, Peter affirms not only that he had found the living stone, precious and chosen by God, but finding it he dedicated his whole life to helping others find it too.

This same change in Peter is what God does in the life of each of his children. Being full of the Spirit doesn't imply that the believer has more of the Holy Spirit. On the contrary, the Holy Spirit has more of the Christian, who has given up his/her selfish desires, to be used by God according to His purposes.

····o **Ask students to complete Activity 5 and then share their answers with the rest of the class.**

||| Then ask them to share their answers with the rest of the class. Invite the students to pray to make a commitment to God to take care of this experience every day, making the changes in their life that will allow them to grow in their relationship with God. |||

Definition of key terms

- **Purity:** a word used to describe the life cleansed of carnality, or inner sin, that drives us to disobey God.

- **Testimony:** This term can mean two things. First, it can be the image that other people have of us. Our testimony to other people depends on how we live our lives. Also, this word can represent an action, to testify. This is when we tell others what has happened in our life or what we've seen happen in someone else's life. We are witnesses of what happened and therefore we can testify on the matter.

Summary

Peter experienced a significant and remarkable change in his life after he was filled with the Spirit of love. He understood that God's will for each of his sons and daughters is to experience His love in their lives and share it with others.

The Holy Spirit infuses power into the life of the believer. This power enables him/her to live in purity, to testify, to serve effectively, and to intercede in prayer for others.

As God's people, we have the task of announcing the hope that's in Christ. But like Peter, we can't do this without first being filled with the Spirit of God's love.

Activity Worksheet

After reading these contemporary examples of nicknames that indicate what the person should become, think of the following: If Jesus gave you a nickname today that would remind you of what you should become, what do you think it would be?

The bulldog

Years ago, a shy boy called Orel, who had an extraordinarily strong and accurate arm, arrived at the smallest baseball league in the United States. The Dodgers coach Tommy Lasorda realized the potential of this young man to become one of baseball's greatest players. However, the young man lacked confidence in himself and a competitive spirit. The coach then gave him a nickname that was the opposite of his personality. He called him "Bulldog". Over time, Orel became one of the most tenacious players in the baseball leagues. His nickname helped him define his attitude and remind him what he could be.

Neo

In the movie "Matrix," the main character is given the new name Neo, which means new, or something old which already exists but had been regenerated. This name reminded him that he was the one chosen to save the human race from the Matrix, and that although he still didn't know it, he had the power to do something special that no one else could do.

My greatest difficulty is _____.

What I should become in God is _____.

Therefore I believe that the nickname suitable for me would be _____.

ACTIVITY 2

What is the work of purification that the Holy Spirit brings to our heart when he fills us?

Complete the following sentences according to what you read in the verses below.

1. John the Baptist said that Jesus has the power to baptize with _____
_____ (Matthew 3:11)

2. Words that describe inner purification are: _____ _____
_____ (1 Corinthians 6:11).

3. By means of _____ we are cleansed (John 15:3).

4. Jesus prayed that we would be _____ (John 17:17).

5. The will of God for our lives is that we grow in _____ (Matthew 5:48).

6. Paul gave us an example of persevering in _____ (Philippians 3:12).

ACTIVITY 3.
What is the difference that marks the full witness of the Spirit? What are the characteristics that give you the power to live the testimony of a person full of the Spirit?

Search the following verses and list the characteristics.

Acts 4:8_____

Acts 4:31 _____

Acts 5:32 _____

Acts 6:5 _____

Acts 6:10 _____

Acts 8:29, 39_____

Acts 10:38_____

ACTIVITY 4.
How does the Spirit guide us in our prayers? Reflect on the next chosen reading by Leslie Parrott under the title of What is Sanctification? (Page 52)

"Praying in the spirit is more than words. Have you prayed with such intensity that you have finally fallen on the bed begging: "O God, I don't know what to say or do. I leave everything in your hands. *In the same way, the Spirit helps us in our weakness. We don't know what we ought to pray for, but the Spirit himself intercedes for us through wordless groans…And we know that in all things God works for the good of those who love him, who have been called according to his purpose.*" (Romans 8:26, 28). The sanctified people learn to leave their life in the hands of God. They are not consumed by restlessness, because they trust in the Lord. They don't criticize, are not whiny, and don't get angry; because they know that even the unfortunate things that happen in the church or in their private life will work for the glory of God. Those who are not fully consecrated cannot have such faith."

ACTIVITY 5.
Read the following anecdote and then evaluate your life by answering the following questions:

"The true witness of the Christian rests not on his words, but on the facts of his life. Missionary doctor and explorer David Livingstone (1813-1873) met in Central Africa with another explorer and writer, Mr. H. M. Stanley (1841-1904) who wasn't a Christian. After a time of traveling together and sharing experiences, Mr. Stanley said, 'If I had stayed with him a little longer, I would have convinced myself to become a Christian; and you know that he didn't tell me about it all.' "

1. Is your life reflecting the life of Christ, or are you still the same person you were before?

_____

_____

_____

2. Have you felt this power of the Spirit acting in your life? How?

_____

_____

_____

3. Would you like to have this kind of life that convinces others to follow Christ because they know you?

_____

_____

_____

4 .What changes do you need to make in your life so that people can notice the life of Christ in you and want to change their lives?

_____

_____

_____

RECOMMENDED READINGS

- Psalm 24
- Psalm 31
- Psalm 51
- Psalm 63
- Matthew 6:38-48
- 1 John 1

Perfect Love: The Lifestyle of the Christian full of the Spirit
Lesson 11

Learning goals:

That the students ...

- Understand the meaning of Christian Perfection from the Divine perspective.
- Reflect on the distinctive qualities of the love of God.
- Identify some of the ways in which God's love is shown in the lives of His children.
- Recognize the evidence of God's love acting in your life.

Resources

- Various types of different seeds, such as beans, coffee, rice, corn, among others
- A small, beautiful and healthy plant in its pot
- An illustration of an adult tree, large and leafy (or one that can be seen from the classroom)
- If you can't get the seeds and the plant, you can get some pictures or illustrative photos.

Introduction

||| Ask students what "lifestyle" means? Write the question on the board and let the students express their ideas. Then write the definition on the board and ask the students to compare it with what they've expressed. "Lifestyle refers to habits, the set of behaviors and attitudes that people develop." |||

Secondly, ask the students to complete Activity 1 and ask two or three students to voluntarily share with the rest what they wrote.

||| Read Ephesians 4:13 together and ask which of the three people they saw in the activity are more likely to reach this goal? |||

When believers are filled with the Holy Spirit, they begin a spiritual walk. Day by day, year by year, they grow and become more secure in Christ. For this to be possible, they must collaborate with the Spirit by making as many life-changes as are necessary to become as Christ-like as possible. In this process, God will completely transform their lives. This change begins in our inner being, as we saw in the last lesson, but as we'll see in this lesson, it becomes more and more evident in what we do.

Bible Study

In this study, we'll define two very important words: love and perfection. The importance of these words is that they summarize what the Spirit-filled Christian lifestyle is. Both words describe the central quality of this ability we receive from God through His Spirit. Both are intimately related in such a way that one quality can't be possible without the other.

In the eyes of God, we can't be perfect if we don't have the love that makes us perfect. Likewise, to love as God loves is required for us to be perfect. We'll begin by defining "perfection".

1. WHAT DOES IT MEAN TO BE PERFECT?

||| Ask for volunteers to read Genesis 17:1 and Matthew 5:48. |||

In both the Old and New Testaments, we find that the call of God to his sons and daughters is to be perfect.

⊙·······◦ **Write on the board: What does "perfect" mean? Divide the class into two groups, one for the ladies and one for the men. Ask the groups to do Activity 2.**

▌▌▌ **Write the ideas expressed by the groups on the board in 2 columns, and then mark the similarities. Secondly, ask each group to write a definition of "What is a perfect fruit?"** ▌▌▌

⊙···········◦ **Ask the students to individually complete Activity 3. Then ask them to share their definitions with the class.**

What does it mean to be perfect from the divine perspective? "Christian Perfection" is one of the names that the experience of the fullness of the Holy Spirit has received in the history of the Church. Some people get confused about what it means to be perfect, stating that it's a life free from flaws, mistakes, attitudes or forms of behavior that may offend in any way. In order to understand the meaning of this word, we'll look at some examples of how Jesus and the disciples used it.

Let's begin with Matthew 5:48. Jesus said, *"Be perfect, therefore, as your heavenly Father is perfect."* What did he mean? If we look at the previous verses from 38-47, Jesus is teaching about how to forgive and love those who have done us some harm. The Greek word that is translated "perfect" in this passage is 'teleios', which means "end, goal or limit." The main teaching in this passage is that the goal for every Christian is to love as God loves us.

Another similar passage is when Jesus is talking with the rich young man and says, *"If you want to be perfect, go, sell your possessions and give to the poor, and you will have treasure in heaven. Then come, follow me"* (Matthew 19:21). The Greek word used is the same 'teleios' from the previous example. Jesus assumed that this young man, like everyone else, wanted to grow and have good goals for his life. But Jesus puts before him a new challenge, a new goal: to love as God loves. And to do so, he needed to put everything else in the background. The teaching here is that the personal goals of the Christian should result in the benefit of other people and not just for himself.

Paul also speaks of perfection in Ephesians 4:13 when he writes to the church, *"... until we all reach unity in the faith and in the knowledge of the Son of God and become mature, attaining to the whole measure of the fullness of Christ."* Paul here uses the same word "teleios," but to describe a perfect person, or in other words, a mature person. In his writings, Paul always urges the brothers to leave their spiritual childhood and reach the goal of maturity. Paul begins this phrase by affirming that each and every believer must reach this goal, and that this is the primary task of the leaders and pastors of the churches.

In 2 Timothy 3:17, Paul also writes, *"... so that the servant of God may be thoroughly equipped for every good work."* Here Paul uses another Greek word 'artios' which translates "perfect" and means "equipped, adjusted or perfectly prepared."

Observing this brief study, we can conclude that in the Bible, the only perfection possible is the perfection of love. Perfect Christians, then, are those who have grown to a point of maturity where they receive the love of God. This perfect love dwelling in their life qualifies them, equips them for service, but at the same time continues to help them become more and more like Jesus.

None of us can be perfect in mind, in understanding, in speaking, or acting until we're in the presence of God. But we can be perfect in love if the river of God's perfect love flows through us. What makes us perfect is not what we do, but the energy of the love of God that dwells in our being. This energy is the one that directs and drives us so that each one of us lives according to the purpose for which we were saved.

> **▌▌▌ To understand better what it means to be perfect, we're going to prove it with these seeds, this plant and this tree. (Show items while giving the explanation that follows). ▌▌▌**

Let's look at these seeds. All of them are different, but in each of them is the potential of becoming a plant or a tree according to their family. Would you say that this seed is perfect? Yes, it's healthy, complete and fulfills its purpose.

Now let's look at the plant. This is a healthy plant. It has everything it needs to grow and multiply. Would you say that this plant is perfect? Yes.

Let's now look this leafy tree. Would you say that it's perfect? Yes, it's healthy, it's complete, it has everything it needs to keep growing and add rings to its trunk. Although it's a large and already an adult tree, it has the ability to reproduce leaves and branches and even grow in height.

These three - seed, plant and tree - are perfect for their stage of development. They're perfect because they're healthy and have everything they need to continue growing and fulfilling the purpose for which God created them. All of them will bear fruit, although the fruit will be different. Some give light to a new life, others are pretty, others give shade, seed, fruit or wood.

In the same way, Spirit-filled Christians are perfect because they're complete. They have the ability to grow in the likeness of Christ and to fulfill the purpose for which God has called each one.

2. WHAT IS PERFECT LOVE LIKE?

○ **Ask the class, What do people understand about love? Then have them do Activity No. 4 of the Activity Worksheet**

Perfect love is that which the apostle Paul describes in 1 Corinthians 13. It's the same love with which Christ loves us. This is a love that is given without reservations, conditions, or measure. It's pure love stripped of selfishness. It's the love that allows us to love God with all our heart, with all our soul, and with our whole mind (Matthew 22:37). This is the love that God fills us with by His Spirit.

The Holy Spirit, filling the heart of the believer, produces a change in the motives and affections that now focus on doing the perfect will of God. This is shown in a new capacity to love God, His work, and all people with an unlimited love, even at the cost of personal sacrifice. It's a love that doesn't seek its own, but always and in everything it seeks to advance the kingdom of God.

Let's look at some of the ways in which perfect love is manifested in the lives of Spirit-filled Christians.

It's intentional love

||| Ask a student to read 1 John 4:19 and ask the class who first loved - God to us or us to Him? |||

Through the Word, we know that God loves us intentionally, that is, He loves us because He has decided to love us, because He wants to love us. The Spirit-filled Christian must not only feel this perfect love, but must make the decision to cultivate that love for God and his fellow man.

With regard to God, Spirit-filled believers put him at the center of their affections. God becomes the number one passion in their life. Spirit-filled Christians strive to please God, just as Jesus did. His only desire, the fundamental purpose of his life, was not to do his own will, but that of his Father (John 6:38). This love is expressed in keeping God's commandments, in our relationship with God, and in loving others as God loves them.

The Greeks used three different words to express love. These words help us to describe the love of God better. Agape love refers to the love that always returns good, even in exchange for evil; Eros love delights in what is beautiful … that which gratifies the senses; Filial love is that which unites in bonds of friendship.

Christians show Agape love in the following ways: they return good for evil when they've been offended (Romans 5:8 and 12:14), and they promote the well-being of others, even those who have harmed them. Christians delight in contemplating the beauty of creation and enjoy what is good, valuable and beautiful. They seek to highlight the beauty of God's creation rather than destroy it, but at the same time they're horrified by the sin that corrupts the world and God's creatures. Christians are faithful friends and promote and cultivate bonds of friendship.

Christians full of the Spirit have the love of God poured into their hearts. They're not just Christians by name, but intentionally seek more of God in their hearts and lives.

It's love that seeks to express itself

||| Ask a student to read John 4:13-14. |||

Jesus compared this abundant fruit of the Spirit with a river of living water flowing within our being. When Jesus spoke of living water, he wanted to emphasize the great difference between a river and a lake. In rivers, the water flows. Its channel empties and refills. Lakes receive the water but accumulate it. In Palestine, there is a lake known as the Dead Sea. It receives the fresh and clean waters of the Jordan River, but instead of distributing them to water the fields, it accumulates them. These waters are so high in salt that nothing can live in them. It's dead water.

The Spirit of God is a force of generous love that runs like fresh water in our lives as Christians, and we can only be fully happy when we spill out our lives in service. With the same intensity with which we love God with all our heart, we serve with all our strength (Acts 24:16). We use our talents and strengths constantly according to our Master's will.

God's abundant Spirit produces abundance of ministry. Perfect love manifests itself in action. God's love mobilizes us. God loves us, and that love led Him to do something for us, for our well-being. Christians who love only in word are not reflecting the genuine love of God.

God wants us to have a proactive love, which is love that seeks the opportunity to express itself instead of sitting waiting to be invited to do something for other people. It's a love that energizes, gives us strength and courage to go wherever the need is. Keeping pews warm is not the sign of real Christians. They're proactive, looking to do all the good that they can. They participate in compassion and evangelism, while sharing the responsibilities of work in the church.

This love is expressed in many different forms and in many different personalities. For example: It's a love that encourages others and rejoices when they're successful. Real love speaks to others about their need to wake up to sin. It leads others to Christ so that they may be justified by faith and have peace with God (Romans 5:1), and encourages those who have accepted Jesus to abound more in love and good deeds.

It's a love that forgives, doesn't hold a grudge or take revenge. It's a love that supports and forgets, forgiving in the same way God has forgiven us in Christ (Colossians 3:13).

It's a love that moves us to give time and money in a sacrificial way, beyond what others may see as rational, much more than any good person would give for a good cause. Spirit-filled Christians are people whose outward life is the reflection of the intimate relationship they have with their Lord.

It's love that transforms our relationships

||| Ask a student to read John 3:34. |||

Jesus said that God wouldn't give his Spirit by measure (little by little), but would pour it out abundantly on each of his sons and daughters. While all Christians must manifest the fruit of the Spirit, the believer full of the Love of God demonstrates abundance in his life.

What's this fruit of the Spirit? Love, joy, peace, patience, kindness, goodness, faithfulness, gentleness and self-control, as Paul wrote in Galatians 5:22-23.

||| Ask a volunteer to read Hebrews 4:1-11. |||

The Spirit-filled life is a peaceful trusting life that is like God's rest on the seventh day after He created the world, and the people of Israel when they finally entered the land of Canaan (Genesis 1:31-2:2). The author of Hebrews says that this rest is only for the people of God, and that it's the result of putting all faith and all trust in our God.

When Christians are filled with the Holy Spirit, the war in their inner being between the life in the flesh and the will of God is finished. Their inner being is no longer divided, they're at peace. Their mind is calm because they have a new assurance that their life depends entirely on God, and finds full happiness doing the will of God.

Spirit-filled Christians are people who are reconciled with God and with themselves, and this is reflected in their relationships with other people. Since there is peace inside, they become peacemakers. Their hearts are clean. They've been purified of all passion of revenge, envy, malice and anger, any ruthless attitude or evil inclination. They've been cleansed of pride and haughtiness that provokes strife (Proverbs 13:10). This perfect love is shown in self-control and humility.

This love as God's love has three important qualities: it's firm, sincere and always seeks the good of the other. It's a love that demands of itself the maximum to give of its best to others. It's a love that does nothing wrong, doesn't support unkindness and doesn't enjoy injustice, shows trust, respect, compassion, is patient, kind and always tells the truth.

Ask the students to complete Activities 5, 6 & 7.

This perfect love becomes the principle that governs or is behind everything we do, including how we relate to other people. The Spirit-filled Christian lifestyle is one that grows in love relationships with other people.

Definition of key terms

- **Perfect love:** is the love of God which His Holy Spirit gives us. This is a love described in 1 Corinthians 13 as a love that gives the best of itself and expects the best of others.

- **Ministry:** Service that a person gives to God and his fellow man.

- **Intentional:** with intention, or purpose of doing something, desiring, willing for something with determination.

- **Delight, enjoyment:** pleasure, satisfaction, feeling satisfied, happy, full.

- **Proactive:** taking the initiative.

Summary

Life in the Spirit is a life of growth in perfect love. It's a life that is increasingly filled with Christ. The abundance of the love of Christ becomes a reality in our lives as believers, transforming our character, habits, attitudes and the way in which we lead our lives and relate to others. This perfect love produces in our life growth that will help us to become mature Christians. The Spirit-filled believer's lifestyle is growth in God's perfect love. This growth is intentional and expressed in a life given in service and in good relationships with others.

Activity Worksheet

ACTIVITY 1

In the following chart, write some differences that you've noticed or learned in these classes between the lifestyle of a non-Christian person, and a Christian living in the flesh, and one who lives full of the Spirit.

Mention examples of: habits, behaviors, attitudes to answer questions.

	Non-Christian	Carnal Christian	Spirit-Filled Christian
Use of free time			
Use of abilities			
Use of possessions			
Relationships with others			

ACTIVITY 2

If your teacher asked you to bring the perfect fruit for the next class, how would you choose it? What would you look for in it? What would be its qualities or characteristics?

_____

_____

_____

ACTIVITY 3

Compare the following definitions of "perfect" taken from different dictionaries with your own ideas and those expressed in class, and then write in your own words a definition of "perfect."

1. Being entirely without fault or defect.

2. Satisfying all requirements

3. Corresponding to an ideal standard or abstract concept.

4. Fulfilling with responsibility and effectiveness the function for which it was designed.

My own definition of perfect is:: _____

_____

ACTIVITY 4
What do people understand about love?

_____

_____

_____

ACTIVITY 5
List some ways you can intentionally show God's love to the following people this week:

To the person I love the most: _____

_____

To the person I find hardest to love: _____

_____

ACTIVITY 6
Respond to the following questions:

1. What valuable experiences do you have in your past history that you can use to serve God?

_____

_____

2. How can God use the experience of your childhood and adolescence?

_____

_____

_____

3. Have you received classes or education, or do you have special talents, or natural or learned skills that can be helpful to God?

_____

_____

_____

4. Is there any painful experience that you've overcome that can be useful to counsel others?

_____

_____

5. Is there any achievement or success you've achieved in your past that you can use to serve the Lord?

_____

_____

ACTIVITY 7
Read the following passages

"... But the fruit of the Spirit's love, joy, peace, forbearance, kindness, goodness, faithfulness, gentleness and self-control. Against such things there is no law " (Galatians 5: 22-23).

"Love is patient, love is kind. It doesn't envy, it doesn't boast, it's not proud. It doesn't dishonor others, it's not self-seeking, it's not easily angered, it keeps no record of wrongs. Love doesn't delight in evil but rejoices with the truth. It always protects, always trusts, always hopes, always perseveres" (1 Corinthians 13:4-7).

What are the areas in which you are conscious that you must grow so that God's love can be shown more fully in your life?

_____

_____

_____

_____

RECOMMENDED READINGS

- 1 John 4
- Romans 15:1-21
- Philippians 4
- Colossians 3
- 1 Thessalonians 5:12-28

Common Mistakes About the Spirit-filled Life
Lesson 12

Learning goals:

That the students ...

- Recognize misconceptions about the evidence of holiness of life.
- Reflect on the danger to the unity of the church of these misguided ways of understanding the Spirit-filled life.
- Share experiences on how these misconceptions affect the testimony of the church in society.
- Propose ideas on how you can help people who are confused to understand what it truly means to live in holiness.

Resources

- Black or white board
- Chalk or markers

Introduction

▌▌▌ Begin the class by writing the following questions on the board. Is it important to know about wrong ideas about the Spirit-filled life? Why and for what purpose will this information be useful to us? Let them express their answers. Summarize each idea and as you speak, make a list on the board. If they don't mention it, you can add: "not to fall into the same mistakes", "to help those who are mistaken", "to defend what the Bible teaches about it", among others. ▌▌▌

Ask the students to complete Activity 1. When they have finished, read each statement and ask the class to say whether the statement is true or false. Then correct them if they are wrong so they can correct their answers on their Activity Worksheets.

In this lesson, we're going to study some of these common mistakes around what it means to be filled with the Spirit and live in holiness.

Bible Study

Some misconceptions about a holy life are:

1. IT DESTROYS OUR FREE WILL

When God created man, he did it to have fellowship with him, to be his friend. Therefore, it's totally wrong to think that the Spirit-filled life annuls our free will, since God never wanted to create robots that respond 'remotely,' or a prisoner who obeys because he is forced to.

We find examples in the Bible by which we can assert that God doesn't destroy free will. Let's review the examples of Adam and Eve and Jesus.

In the case of Adam and Eve, God created them and made them responsible for administering Eden, but at no time did He make them obey him by force. In Genesis 2:8-9, we find God putting man in the Garden of Eden, and we also find that He gave them the tree of the knowledge of good and evil. This really represents the opportunity to choose. Of course, God makes his recommendation to us human beings, but doesn't force our decisions. Notice the decision of the first couple in Genesis 3:6, "When the woman saw that the fruit of the tree was good for food and pleasing to the eye, and also desirable for gaining wisdom, she took some and ate it. She also gave some to her husband, who was with her, and he ate it." Adam and Eve chose a fatal option for their lives, resulting in separation from their Creator.

Let's look at the example of Jesus.

▌▌▌ Ask a student to read Luke 22:39-44. ▌▌▌

In this passage, we find the Lord choosing to obey the will of his Father, however difficult it might have been, and Jesus expressed his desire to the Father. It wasn't easy for Him to go to the cross, to sacrifice himself, to gain enemies, to pay the price of solitude, of being misunderstand, to receive insults, physical abuse and even death. Jesus wasn't forced to go to the cross. He went of his own free will, out of love for his Father and out of love for us. That's why he prays for strength to fulfill the will of his Father to the end.

As we can see, free will isn't destroyed in the life of the Spirit-filled person. In the Christian life, we'll always have to make decisions, and God is pleased that his children obey him of their own choice.

2. BEING FILLED WITH THE SPIRIT MAKES US IMMUNE TO TEMPTATION

This is also a misconception since we find that the holy Son of God was tempted to the extreme.

||| Ask a student to read Matthew 4:1-11. |||

In Matthew 4 we read how the Lord was tempted three times. In the first, Satan takes advantage of the basic human need for food, since Jesus had spent 40 days fasting. In the second, he was tempted to prove the faithfulness of his Father, and in the third he was tempted with riches and power. Hebrews 4:15 (VP) tells us that Jesus *"... may have compassion for our weakness, because He also was subject to the same trials as we; only that he never sinned."*

In the Scriptures, we find many examples of people who failed to overcome or emerge victorious from temptation, such as Ananias and Sapphira, whose story is told in Acts 5:1-11. This Christian couple was tempted in the area of money. They decided to try to deceive the apostles so as to appear generous. But they were lying, since they were keeping part of the amount of the sale of their property. Peter reminds Ananias that they weren't required to sell their land, or to hand over the money from the sale to the church (Acts 5:4). Sin consisted in not being honest with God, whom no one can deceive (Galatians 6:7). The consequence of this attitude was deadly.

We can't avoid being tempted, but we can pray for God to help us triumph over temptation.

Ask the students to complete Activity 2.

In the same way as the father in the illustration in Activity 2, the Spirit-filled person can "technically" sin. As we have seen, he is not free from temptation. The fact is that he does not want to sin because he loves his Lord so much that he does not want to do anything that He dislikes. He has been delivered from the desire to consciously do evil, out of his love for the one who loved him first and gave himself for him on the cross.

3. THAT IT WILL GIVE US INSTANT MATURITY

Don't confuse purity with maturity. There's a difference between a person who has been filled with the Spirit for one day and one who has been filled by the Spirit for ten years. Both have the same level of purity, but not the same level of maturity. The path to spiritual maturity is a process of 'growth' in an intimate relationship with Jesus. We need to grow in Bible study, obedience to the Word and in fellowship and service in the church.

When someone gets their first driver's license (usually when they are young), it enables them to drive a vehicle. But this new driver will have to learn skills, such as knowledge of the roads, how to react to an improper maneuver of another driver, the ability to change a tire, and the expertise in the basic upkeep of his automobile. There will be a difference between a new driver and a person who has been driving for years. Both of their driving licenses will be the same, and both will have passed a driving test satisfactorily. The difference is that one license is new, and the license of the other driver has been renewed several times and he has gained experience with the passing of the years. So, it is with purity and maturity.

An example of purity, and at the same time immaturity in a person, can be seen in the life of the apostle Peter.

||| Read Galatians 2:11-14. |||

Peter was a person filled with the Holy Spirit who acted hypocritically by failing to share with non-Jewish believers for fear of what other church leaders would think of him. Paul rebukes Peter for his immature attitude and for associating with those who demanded that the 'gentile' Christians pass through the rite of circumcision (a Jewish custom that came from the time of Moses) before being accepted into the church.

4. THAT IT MAKES US ALL THE SAME

Each of us has been created unique. Even identical twins physically speaking have differences in how they are. Science has shown that there are different types of temperaments that we have when we're born. Some people say that there are four basic temperaments: choleric, sanguine, phlegmatic and melancholy. Each of these has its own characteristics that will make us prefer certain things over others, be more or less extroverted, react differently to the same situation, and so on. Holiness doesn't destroy the personality we have. Although experience is transforming us into the image of Christ, we will preserve our unique characteristics.

This we see clearly reflected in the life of the apostles, even after Pentecost, when they were filled with the Spirit. Think of a moment in the lives of Peter, John or Paul. What were the characteristics of the personality of these men before they were filled with the Holy Spirit? What changes occurred? Were these changes beneficial to their task?

There are those who think that a deeper encounter with the Lord, Pentecost in the case of Peter and John, and Damascus in Paul's case, may perhaps have accentuated their personalities and may have added value for the faithful fulfillment of God's mission charge.

For example, Peter was always the bold one who took the initiative to speak out in the gospels. In Acts, we see this same characteristic, only with a deeper degree of commitment. We often observe John near Jesus, someone whom Jesus loved in a special way. In his letters, we find a tender apostle calling the brothers, "My little children." Finally, in Paul we find someone who before his conversion was categorical in his convictions and extremely zealous of fulfilling the law. His writings reflect an apostle with direct language concerned that the churches should live according to the gospel of grace.

||| Ask the class, 'Can God take advantage of our natural temperaments and use them for the fulfillment of the mission entrusted to us? How? Can you give some examples?' |||

5. THAT WE'LL BE PERFECT LIKE THE GOOD ANGELS

In a congregation when there are differences of opinion and problems among believers, this proves that the work of the Kingdom is developing among human beings. The only place where there are no conflicts at all is in a cemetery. There only the dead remain, and dead people don't have differences of opinion, they don't have agendas or interests. If we're alive, we'll have conflicts. Where there's a group of human beings, there will be problems to be solved.

Holiness doesn't prevent us from making mistakes with people or making wrong decisions, or thinking differently from others or offending others for some reason, or being offended by something that someone has said or done.

Paul and Barnabas had a difference of opinion about John Mark, which led them to separate as fellow travelers. However, because they were still filled with the Spirit, this didn't turn them away from the missionary ministry they had received from God.

People who are being sanctified by God will never reach the degree of perfection of the good angels, who are free of all our human imperfections. We're in the world to be salt and light. To be salt by imparting life to society and preserving it from evil, and being light by leading others on the path of salvation (Matthew 5:13-16). As long as we continue to fulfill our mission in this life, we'll never be free from human error and weakness.

However, as we saw in point 3, we must grow every day in order to be more and more like Christ. If, for example, at the beginning of our walk in the Spirit ,we were strongly affected by the comments and attitudes of others. But after several years, we'll find that they don't harm us, and it becomes easier to forgive and forget the offense immediately. If years ago we judge with ease the intentions of other people, then we must learn that this is the Lord's task. If in the past, we made decisions hurriedly that could harm people or things, today we pray and meditate more, exploring all possibilities to seek the option of what God really wants. Even so, we'll never be exempt from making mistakes, as long as we're in this world.

6. THAT WE CAN DO WHATEVER WE LIKE

Living in the fullness of the Spirit, we have freedom, not freedom to sin, but freedom to obey our God in a better way without any hindrances that limits our complete surrender to Him.

We're not free to live as we like in the selfish old way, but we chose freely to submit ourselves to the sweet and tender love of our Lord Jesus Christ, to serve Him with our whole being (1 Peter 2:16). If we allow our self-centered desires to dominate us, then we're their slaves. But if we do the will of our heavenly Father, then we're set free by the power of Jesus (Romans 6:1,2; Galatians 5:1).

Freedom isn't permission to do what I please to do. That's called debauchery. Freedom means having the ability to do what I should do.

7. IT IS CONFUSED WITH LEGALISM

Sometimes, in the process of entire consecration that precedes the fullness of the Spirit, God deals with some areas of our life (sometimes one or two) which we find harder to surrender. When these things are finally left on the altar, the Lord responds with his sanctifying work in our lives. The problem is that we often think that since these were critical areas for us, they should be for all people. We could become legalists if we try to impose on others the change of those specific 'things' as a requirement to be filled with the Spirit.

Let's look at an example. David is a person who before knowing the Lord followed a particular music band as his 'god.' He bought all their CDs, went to all their concerts, etc. In the process of his consecration, the Lord indicated that it would be better to get rid of all the CDs, posters and magazines of that band that he had at home. That was necessary in his case, to be filled with the sanctifying presence of Jesus. David never wanted to return to listen to this music because for him it represented a return to the past, to a life without Christ. At present, he only listens to Christian music. The radio of his car is only tuned to an evangelical station.

James, on the other hand, who goes to the same local church, has in his house some records of that same band and also some Christian music that he also listens to. Every now and then he enjoys listening to a song sung by that band, where the lyrics are not offensive to God or the Bible. For James, who's also filled with the Holy Spirit, that music wasn't a problematic area in his total surrender to the Lord. The band wasn't his 'god' nor will it ever be. Therefore, it doesn't affect his spiritual growth to listen to some of their music. If David tries to convince James that he can't be truly filled with God's presence unless he gets rid of all that music, he will have fallen into a legalistic attitude.

Decades ago, in some Christian churches, legalism had to do with the kind of clothing that women could wear, or the use of marriage rings for men, among others. Much more attention was paid to the 'outward form' of living holiness than to that of the heart (Colossians 2:11).

Legalism often begins innocently when we want to establish rules to avoid 'worldly' behavior or to demand certain practices as a requirement to grow in faith or to be welcomed in the church. The consequences of legalism can be very serious. Many people, and even children of believers, have moved away from the church because of it. We'll do well to listen to the words of the apostle Paul in 2 Corinthians 3:6, *"... He has made us competent as ministers of a new covenant—not of the letter but of the Spirit; for the letter kills, but the Spirit gives life. "*

8. IT IS SIMPLY EMOTIONALISM

In our day, and as a consequence of a society increasingly hungry for 'strong' emotions, the desire for emotionalism is probably more noticeable than ever before.

Obviously, human beings are naturally emotional, and there is nothing wrong with expressing our emotions. In fact, it's neither possible nor healthy to have a relationship with God that lacks emotion. However, we may fall into the error that emotional manifestations occupy the main place in our spiritual life.

When we say that God is with us because we 'feel good,' or when we measure our level of spirituality by 'how much we enjoy today's service,' we're showing obvious signs of emotionalism. The interesting thing is that sometimes believers, in a state of emotional overflow, may not know what we're saying, like Peter on the mountain of transfiguration (Luke 9: 33-36).

It's necessary to emphasize that all of us respond emotionally to spiritual experiences. However, the way we respond is determined by our temperament, our past experiences, and the environment in which we develop. In services, some people raise one or both hands to heaven with closed eyes. Others clap or shout "amen." Another will only say "thank you Lord" in a low voice or shed some tears. We can't make "laws" one way or another about how one should respond to the presence of the Lord.

Keith Drury says that "Emotionalism can be misleading ... an attractive drift away from the central truth of holiness ... induces people to seek a 'spiritual drunkenness,' or certain sensations. Emotions can be excited by preaching, by singers, or by musical ensembles, resulting in a false sense of God's blessing while, in truth, it's a superficial disguise of what is true."

Mixing faith with emotions isn't a new phenomenon. It has happened before in the history of the church. In Christian congregations at different times, some emotional manifestations have been associated with the presence of God, or even with the fullness of the Holy Spirit.

Some of these manifestations linked to spirituality have been the following:

1. A new language of prayer

2. Shaking or falling in the Spirit

3. Explosions of laughter, shouting, running or other expressions of emotions.

4. Instant spiritual knowledge or revelation, so that theological education is unnecessary

5. Process of "inner healing" in counseling, which minimizes the Lord's purifying work at the altar.

○ **Organize the class to complete Activity 3. Divide the class into groups of two. Half of the groups will work on "legalism" and the other half on "emotionalism." Then suggest a time of sharing of each group's discussion, beginning with those of the "legalism" group, and then with those of "emotionalism," so that both groups can share their ideas about each topic.**

End the class with a prayer of thanksgiving to God for the good teaching of our Church of the Nazarene, which helps us to get onto the path of spiritual maturity, which is God's will for our life, revealed in Jesus Christ.

[1] Drury, Keith. *Holiness for all Believers.* Indiana, Wesleyan Publishing House: 1995, p. 47.

Definition of key terms

- **Debauchery:** excessive indulgence in sensual pleasures. Some people misrepresent the concept of freedom in Christ and feel that they can now do what they like, satisfying themselves without any restriction. These people don't submit to the will of God.

- **Legalism:** an excessive adherence to law or formula. Legalistic people strictly adhere to certain moral codes or laws, without admitting any variation. This can turn into fanaticism where people lose mercy and consideration in dealing with other people.

- **Free will:** The power to choose between two or more options and be responsible for the decisions they make, and their consequences.

- **Angelic perfection:** Good angels are servants of God who don't sin. They are not like God, but are superior to human beings. By this perfection, the angels fulfill the will of God with exactitude and with a deep love.

- **Emotionalism:** Overflow of emotions often confused with a high level of spirituality or with the experience of the fullness of the Holy Spirit. Emotionalism has had different expressions throughout history.

Summary

Around us there are many different ways of understanding the life of holiness and the experience of the fullness of Holy Spirit. Some are biblically correct and some are wrong. Many confuse holiness with emotionalism, legalism, debauchery, being perfect, being immune to temptation and other things. Identifying these mistakes will help us not to fall into them, and will keep us focused on continuing to grow in the holy life as the Spirit teaches us to live closer to the love of God and further away from sin each day.

Activity Worksheet

ACTIVITY 1
Here are some statements about the holy life. Indicate with F the ones you consider false and with T the true ones.

The sanctified person ...

___Has free will (can chose to sin or not)

___Is immune to temptation

___ Receives instant maturity when filled with the Holy Spirit.

___Can think differently and disagree on things with others who are sanctified.

___Becomes the same as the angels

___Raises their hands to worship

___Never argues with another Christian

___Laughs all the time

___Speaks in a strange language to pray

___doesn't need to go to the altar to pray

ACTIVITY 2
Reflect on the following and respond.

Think of a parent about 40 years old. His wife has just had a beautiful son after many years of not being able to conceive, and the nurse brings it to the father to hold in his arms for the first time.

Do you think that father will kill his son? Does he have the strength to do it? Does he have the means available?

The answer to all these questions will be obvious. 'He can technically', but ... Will the father kill his son?

Why do you think he wouldn't?

_____

_____

ACTIVITY 3
Discuss in group the following questions:

1. Are there still some of the aforementioned forms of legalism /emotionalism around us?

_____

_____

_____

2. What other modern expressions of legalism /emotionalism have we come across?

_____

_____

_____

3. What can we do about it?

_____

_____

_____

RECOMMENDED READINGS

- Romans 7:7 - 8:17
- Colossians 3
- 1 Timothy 1
- 1 Timothy 4:1-16
- 2 Timothy 2:14-26

SETTING GOALS FOR MY SPIRITUAL LIFE
Lesson 13

Learning goals:

That the students will...

- Understand that they must take responsibility for their spiritual growth.
- Reflect on the ways in which Christians persevere in the Spirit-filled life.
- Measure their current state of vulnerability to temptation.
- Evaluate their spiritual growth up to now.
- Propose new goals for their spiritual life in the next six months.

Resources

- A photo of a vine
- A vine branch (if possible)
- Fresh grapes or grape juice
- Disposable cups and serviettes for each student

Introduction

In this lesson, we're going to study what the Word of God tells us about the Christian's responsibility to care for and grow in the experience of the fullness of the Spirit. As we've studied in the lessons of this quarter, God saves us so that we may live lives full of his Spirit and have a lifestyle of perfect love.

In order to live in this experience of holiness and grow in it, it's very important that we understand well our responsibility to collaborate with the Spirit in the work of restoration that has begun in our life. What are the dangers that threaten our healthy spiritual growth?

As in the previous lessons, we'll try to give you some practical help.

Bible Study

Me ... Holy? What does the life of a person living full of God's holy love look like? Let's look at an illustration that will help us better understand this idea.

A little boy went on holiday to Europe with his family. They toured several cities and some of the largest and awe-inspiring churches that man has ever built. A few months later in his Sunday School class, his teacher asked, "What is a saint?" The boy thought for a moment and remembered the great beauty of the immense stain-glass windows of those cathedrals with their crystals of varied colors and said, "A saint is a person who lets the light of God pass through him."

This child expressed the concept of holiness in a few words with great richness of meaning. The holy life is one that's transparent and clean, which allows the life of Christ to be shown in its entire splendor; someone who does their best to love, to heal, to teach and to bring the light of salvation to all.

As we said in the introduction, we're going to see some things we must do to grow healthily in the life of perfect love.

▌▌▌ Ask a student to read John 15: 1-17. ▌▌▌

In this teaching that Jesus gave his disciples, we can find the keys to our permanence and growth in the life of love. Let's see what they are:

1. KEEP YOUR LIFE CENTERED ON JESUS CHRIST

||| Read again verse 4 of John 15. Show the images
of the vine as you continue the lesson. |||

Jesus says that to remain in the spiritual life, we must be like the branch of the vine. Branches have nothing to do but stick to the trunk and bear fruit. Their responsibility is limited to receiving the sap and nutrition that the trunk brings from the roots. Contrary to what some believe, the Spirit-filled life only requires living connected to the source of life. Nothing can replace this intimate communion with Jesus. Some inadvertently substitute this for work in ministry, or other legitimate occupations of life. That is, they are more concerned about bearing much fruit than with being united to the Lord of the fruit.

But if we meditate earnestly on what the Bible says, we'll realize that the fruit won't give us the necessary nutrients to keep us alive spiritually. If you take a group of grapes or take a glass of grape juice and put them beside a branch of the vine, what will happen?

If we look at the results of our work, at our achievements and triumphs, we run the risk of believing the source of spirituality is the fruit. After all, we can say, "Was I not the branch that bore the fruit?" That's why our first responsibility is to keep ourselves filled with the Spirit to remain united to Jesus Christ.

2. GROWING IN WORSHIP AND KEEPING HUMBLE

The life of the Spirit-filled Christian is of absolute dependence on God. This is the basis of worship. True worshipers humble themselves in spirit and recognize that their whole life, and the life of all that surrounds them, comes from the hand of God. They recognize that the vine does all the work that guarantees its growth so that it can continue to bear fruit.

In a town in London, called Hampton Court, there is a grapevine which is famous because sometimes it reaches a million clusters. For a long time, the secret of its productivity was a mystery until somebody resolved the matter. Near this place where the vine is planted, the waters of the River Thames flow by, and the roots of the vine travel more than a hundred meters to feed on the water and the rich nutrients that the river has. The roots carry all the food to the trunk; the vine does all the work and the branches receive the benefit.

If you cut a branch of this vine, it will become a dry stick that's only good for firewood (John 15:6). The Holy Spirit is the one who holds us to the source of life, which is Christ. Separated from him, we can do nothing. Moreover, everything we do, when we teach, when we testify, when we serve, everything depends on Him and the flow of His Spirit, which is the sap that nourishes our life.

Spirit-filled Christians must always recognize that their life is nothing without the nourishment of the Lord.

3. KEEP YOUR MIND CENTERED ON CHRIST WITH A POSITIVE ATTITUDE

John 15:11 says that if we live united to the vine, we'll have the joy of Jesus dwelling in our being. Joy is one of the fruit that the Holy Spirit brings to our life. However, if we don't take care of it and protect it, it can leave our lives.

One of the greatest problems affecting Christians is the loss of joy. This can happen for many reasons, like being treated badly, having fear or insecurity for the future, financial problems or lack of work, seeing a bad testimony in other Christians, stress or depression produced by excessive work, ingratitude toward others for their service to the Lord, being a victim of some situation or unfair treatment on the part of brothers and sisters in the church, among others.

All of these problems can take away our joy, especially if we have the idea that the Christian life is an easy life. Christians who put their hope in circumstances and in people will soon be disappointed, because people are not perfect and life is not a holiday.

The only way to persevere in the joy of the Lord is to keep our mind centered on Jesus Christ.

Nothing is further from the Spirit-filled life than a bitter Christian. A person with bitterness lives full of rancor, feels self-pity, is complaining, moody, always looking for defects in people and in what people do. On the other hand, Spirit-filled Christians cast out negative thoughts and don't allow them to take root in their heart.

To maintain this positive mind, we must learn to be grateful in everything and for everything to God and to others. This means that we must still be grateful for the difficulties, because it's in the midst of them that we most need to cling to the trunk from which our hope feeds. Christians grow in joy when they learn to bless. To bless means to give words of peace, of forgiveness, of acceptance. The Spirit wants to teach us to carry our thoughts along the path of blessing, and use our mouths as a tool of blessing, rejecting every sinful habit of speaking negatively.

4. DO NOT STOP FEEDING YOURSELF

⦀ Read John 15:7. ⦀

The sap running through the trunk that brings the nutrients into our lives is this wonderful partnership of the Holy Spirit and the Word of God. When the Spirit fills us, He puts in our lives the desire to know more of the Lord God, and encourages us to go much deeper into the Word of God. All of this leads to greater growth and a stronger more solid Christian life. However, for this to be possible, Christians must discipline themselves, devoting time and effort to study, and maintaining healthy habits such as attending worship services, going to Bible study classes, enjoying friendship and conversation with brothers and sisters in the faith, helping to disciple others, studying the Word alone and in groups, and perfecting themselves in the practice of their gifts for ministry. All of this will help us grow healthily.

Here we must warn that spiritual growth should not be equated with intellectual knowledge. The growth of the Christian doesn't consist only in learning certain information about the Bible. Some people may come to know a lot about God, but in reality, they don't know Him or serve Him with their lives. Intellectual knowledge carries within itself the danger of enlightenment which only builds pride, but this alone doesn't change the way we live (Matthew 7:16, Ephesians 5:8, James 2:18).

We don't mean that knowledge is bad. On the contrary, we affirm that it's good when we understand that it's only the first step in progress towards maturity. To grow in our spiritual life, we also need to go through a variety of experiences like worship, fellowship, and study, and put into practice in our life what has been learned. Spiritual growth forms our character and our vision, and provides us with skills for ministry.

In Philippians 3:13-14, the apostle Paul says, *"... I don't consider myself yet to have taken hold of it. But one thing I do: Forgetting what is behind and straining toward what is ahead, I press on toward the goal to win the prize for which God has called me heavenward in Christ Jesus."* The path to Christian maturity must be followed throughout our lives. As we move forward, we can recognize what we need, and then take action to remedy it. To grow in holiness of life, it's imperative to recognize before God that we need Him to reach the goal. This humble attitude is necessary for us to be formed through Scriptures and our Christian leaders and teachers.

This process of growth goes on for the rest of a person's life. That is why in the church we're all disciples, even the leaders who are in positions of greater responsibility. Remember that the spiritual growth of the Christian is intentional and not automatic (Acts 5:12, Philippians 2:12, Romans 6:13).

To live life full of the Holy Spirit, it's essential to continue getting nourishment in the best possible way to grow strong and healthy in this new life.

▐▐▐ Distribute the grapes. You can say something like this: The sweetest grapes are those that mature while on the vine. In the same way, the life of the Christian who feeds himself connected to Jesus Christ transmits sweetness to the people around him. Ask the class: How would you like to be remembered? Like a sour grape or a sweet grape? ▐▐▐

5. OBEY THE LORD AT ALL TIMES AND IN ALL PLACES

⬢ ·······o Ask the students to get in groups of 2 and answer the questions in Activity 1. Then tell them that those who succeeded in #5 are those who pointed out as true: "Holiness of heart is only possible through a disciplined life."

This is what the apostle Peter wanted to teach in 1 Peter 1:13 when he says, *"with minds that are alert and fully sober."* The King James' version says *"gird up the loins of your mind."* This figure reminds us of the Oriental custom of tying the tunic with a belt in preparation for action. What the apostle Peter is saying here is that it's our responsibility to make the decision to put into practice the teachings of the Word of God in our lives.

As we see, the life of obedience is the normal life of the disciple of Christ. In 1 Peter 1:15, Peter writes, *"But just as he who called you is holy, so be holy in all you do."* A journalist asked Mother Teresa of Calcutta, "What do you think about the fact that people say that you're a saint?" She answered: "I don't see why they see me as extraordinary; saints are what we all should be. God has created us and so it's the most natural thing that must happen in the life of every human being!"

Living in holiness is not an option; it's a call and a vocation for all Christians.

Peter ends by saying *"in all you do."* Where and when should we live in perfect obedience to God's will for our lives? The biblical answer is that we must be completely obedient. This refers to public life and private life. It includes motives, desires, feelings, attitudes, what we say, what we think and what we do.

In our life, there is a dimension that others can see, and another one very intimate that only God and us know about. The most difficult obedience for Christians is that which has to do with their private lives. There we're alone with our thoughts, our desires and our motivations. But when we remain pure and obedient in our private lives, the results are plain to see when we're with others.

Some Christians try to maintain a double life. They may achieve it for a while, but sooner or later, the spiritual lack of life is noticed in their lives. It's not possible to live life full of the Holy Spirit and serve in the church, and at the same time live just as we like in our private lives. This causes many problems, not only for the person trying to live the double life, but it also damages the testimony of the church, and can keep the children of those believers from following the Lord's way.

The great challenge for us is to live in complete purity and obedience before God, ourselves and our neighbors.

6. RESIST TEMPTATIONS

There are no vaccines against temptation, and no Christian is free of them. Satan targets Spirit-filled Christians. His most common strategy is to make them doubt the Word of God and their spiritual progress. Let's look at some examples.

Ask the students to complete Activity 2.

Temptations come again and again, even in the lives of people who are serving God with their lives. The most dangerous temptations are those that attack us at times when we're most vulnerable (Jesus tempted Satan when he was tired and hungry).

Any Christian can fall into temptation, even the one who is filled with the Holy Spirit. Usually they won't be huge sins - a bad thought, a bad decision, an offensive word, losing patience, an expression of pride, among others. These little sins can represent those dangerous cracks through which we slip and fall into an abyss of deeper sin.

To avoid this, it's important to remember that the Holy Spirit warns us of the danger of temptation, and we need to seek God's strength to resist in prayer. If we fall, it's best to immediately ask for God's forgiveness, and forgiveness from anybody else we have hurt. Just like the vine dresser prunes the vineyard, the Spirit-filled Christian needs their life to be kept clean all the time.

We all go through stages of weakness in our lives, where we're most vulnerable to temptation. As far as we can, we must avoid entering these dangerous areas, although it won't always be possible. For example, Christians sometimes work too much. We have work responsibilities at home, with the family, in the church and many add and add commitments to their agendas to the point of not having a moment of rest. In the following self-examination, we'll see, for example, that being exhausted physically and mentally makes us open to temptations.

⬤·····○ Ask the students to complete Activity 3, and once they have worked out their sensitivity to temptation, ask them to share the interpretation of their scores.

7. HAVE CLEAR GOALS

How do you become a saint in every way you live?

▌▌▌ Ask a student to read aloud Philippians 3:13-14. ▐▐▐

In the Christian life, if we don't advance, we deteriorate. The key is to never stop growing. Paul says, "... *But one thing I do: Forgetting what is behind and straining toward what is ahead, I press on toward the goal to win the prize for which God has called me heavenward in Christ Jesus.*"

Who said that the Christian life is boring? On the contrary, the Christian life is one that always presents us with new challenges, new spiritual mountains to climb, and new seas of knowledge to navigate. To the intellectual, Jesus Christ is an inexhaustible source of knowledge. For the practical person, Jesus Christ is the God who every day surprises us with small miracles. For the artist, God is the author of inexhaustible wonders. For the romantic, God is the source of love. The Christian life is a life where there is always something better and wonderful that God has for us.

This passage teaches us the value of having goals in life. Achieving a goal requires determination. The Christian who achieves the goal is the one who doesn't surrender to difficulties. We must be clear that salvation and Christian perfection is by faith, but growth depends on our continuing to the goal of maturity to which the Spirit is guiding us.

Goals in our spiritual life help us to avoid the following dangers: stagnation, mediocre Christian life and conformism. Goals help us to get closer to God, to know Christ more, to depend more on Him, and to become more and more like Him every day.

⬤·····○ Finish the class with Activities 4, 5, & 6.

Definition of key terms

- **Temptation:** stimulus that induces one to do wrong. It can come from our own inner bad desires or from the circumstances that arise in life and that awaken those desires.

- **Goal:** the object of a person's ambition or effort; an aim or desired result; something that they are trying to do or achieve.

- **Humility:** a modest or low view of one's own importance; attitude of the person who doesn't brag about his achievements, recognizes his failures and weaknesses, and acts without pride.

Summary

The permanence of the Christian in the Spirit-filled life depends on his own commitment and obedience by remaining united to Jesus and keeping far away from sin. There is no vaccine against temptation. Sanctified believers also experience temptation, but rely on the help of the Holy Spirit to recognize and defeat it. If believers sin, it's very important that they repent and not remain in sin. The formation of the life of Christ in the Christian demands that we have clear goals for our spiritual growth, and discipline ourselves to attain them. There are always new goals to aid us to grow in the Spirit-filled life.

Activity Worksheet

ACTIVITY 1
Read 1 Peter 1:13-16 and respond to the following questions.

1. What kind of children does God want us to be?

_____

2. What kind of desire do people have who haven't been born again?

_____

3. What makes people live in sin, satisfying the desires of the flesh?

_____

4. Who calls us to be saints and why?

_____

5. How is it possible to remain holy and pure in our hearts? Choose the option you consider to be true:

___ Holiness of heart remains even if we commit sin.

___ Holiness of heart is only possible through a disciplined life.

___ Holiness of heart is God's responsibility not ours.

___ Holiness of heart is only possible for those who have entered into their eternal abode.

ACTIVITY 2
Is your life of holiness being attacked by temptations? Point out in this list the thoughts that have come to your life in recent weeks.

___ Belief that your life of holiness of heart totally depends on your effort.

___ You think that you're better than others because of your life of holiness of heart.

___ Feeling that you deserve privileges because of your purity of heart and life.

___ You demand acknowledgment and congratulations for your life of holiness of heart.

___ You seek your own self-satisfaction with your life of holiness of heart without giving glory to God.

___ You forget that others need help to achieve their holiness of heart.

___ You don't need to continue the development of your experience of holiness of heart.

ACTIVITY 3
Do the following self examination to measure your state of vulnerability to temptation.[1]

At every moment of our life, we find ourselves at different levels of sensitivity to temptation. The following self-examination will help you measure how your sensitivity is now. Each of these ten categories starts with a more negative end and goes through an ascending scale from 1 to 10 to reach the more positive side.

Circle the number that identifies you in each category with regard to where you are now:

1.	Physically exhausted / tired	1-2-3-4-5-6-7-8-9-10	Energetic / Strong
2.	Emotionally discouraged / depressed	1-2-3-4-5-6-7-8-9-10	Encouraged / Stimulated
3.	Mentally bored /Unhappy	1-2-3-4-5-6-7-8-9-10	Excited / Content
4.	Spiritually exhausted /Empty	1-2-3-4-5-6-7-8-9-10	Satisfied / Full
5.	Geographically distant /alone	1-2-3-4-5-6-7-8-9-10	Near / United
6.	Distant from others / Cold	1-2-3-4-5-6-7-8-9-10	Nearby / Warm
7.	Inwardly pessimistic / sad	1-2-3-4-5-6-7-8-9-10	Optimistic / happy
8.	Unconfident at the personal level / Unsafe	1-2-3-4-5-6-7-8-9-10	Safe / Confident
9.	Bitter in secret / Bad temper	1-2-3-4-5-6-7-8-9-10	Forgiving / tolerant
10.	Deeply resentful / Hurt	1-2-3-4-5-6-7-8-9-10	Appreciated / Beloved
	My total today is:		

Interpretation of scores

Healthy area

90-100   You're not in this world; you're already in heaven with God!

80-89   You're very strong, but maybe you should be careful about pride and arrogance

70-79   Be strong, keep up your dependence on the Lord

60-69   You are on the right track, keep obeying the Lord

---

[1] Adapted from Bruce Wilkinson. *Personal Health in Moments of Temptation*. Miami: Unilit, 1998, pp. 157-158.

Area of danger

50-59	You're weak and emotionally vulnerable. Ask others to pray for you for strength
30-49	You're in danger! Protect yourself well because you're weak. Find a Christian friend of the same sex for help.

Crisis zone

20-29	The situation is critical. Possibly you have already given in to some serious sin. Seek help from a Christian counselor and repent.
1-19	Are you breathing? Can you move your body? You need to be born again, because your life is not that of a disciple of Christ.

ACTIVITY 4.

The following is an example list of attitudes that the Christian can have in his life. Some of them are positive and favor your spiritual growth, while others are negative in the sense that they keep you stuck and stop your growth. Evaluate how your life currently is in each aspect with the following table:

1 = never, 2 = sometimes, 3 = half the time, 4 = almost always, and 5 = always.

Column A

____ I mourn for the failures in my past.
____ I forget the mistakes I make.
____ I don't notice much change in my life.
____ I get bored in worship services.
____ I have no real friends who are Christians.
____ I give offerings because I'm supposed to.
____ I don't agree so much about loving others.
____ I have plenty of time to become a mature Christian.
____ I don't have time to work in the church.
____ I criticize my pastor and my leaders.
____ If I like something I'll wear it.
____ People should tolerate my character because God made me like this
____ I know too much about this.
____ My achievements are due to my abilities.
____ I'm the ruler in my house.

Column B

____ I look at the future with hope.
____ I learn from my mistakes.
____ I try to live out everything I learn.
____ I go to the church services with enthusiasm.
____ I have good friends at church.
____ Giving is a privilege.
____ I worry about growing in love.
____ I want to be a mature Christian.

____ I enjoy working in the church.
____ I thank God for my pastor and leaders.
____ I am careful in the way I dress.
____ I ask for forgiveness if I say or do something wrong.
____ I have more to learn about this.
____ I owe my achievements to the Lord.
____ In my house, Jesus is the Lord.

Note: If you often have attitudes in column A, these are not favoring your growth. If you have more in column B, carry on, you're showing signs of growth and maturity in your Christian life.

ACTIVITY 5
The following questions will help you evaluate your spiritual development so far. Answer Yes or No.

___ Can you say that you know God more now than you did two months ago?

___ Have the biblical principles you've learned changed anything in your life these past few weeks?

___ Do you spend time every day reading the Word of God and meditating on it?

___ Do the times you dedicate to pray, both alone as well as at church, give you strength and edify your life, your family, and your congregation?

___ Has your family noticed the changes that Christ has produced in your character?

___ Have your friends and neighbors noticed that you're a Christian because of your lifestyle?

___ Do you need to know and grow more in your Christian experience?

___ Do you consider that you know enough to help others?

___ Do you seek the guidance of God to make decisions for your life and that of your family?

___ If you're married, have you been a better companion for your spouse?

___ Do you regularly attend church services?

___ Do you use your gifts by volunteering in church ministries?

___ Do you give the tithe of all your income? Do you give generously?

ACTIVITY 6.

Write goals for your spiritual growth in the next six months. You can see your weak areas in the results of Activity 4 and 5. Pray and ask the Holy Spirit to show you those areas where you need the most growth.

1. For my relationship with God

_____

_____

_____

_____

2. For my relationship with my family

_____

_____

_____

_____

3. For my relationship with my brothers and sisters in Christ.

_____

_____

_____

_____

4. For my testimony to the world

_____

_____

_____

_____

RECOMMENDED READINGS

- Galatians 5:1-15
- Ephesians 5:1-33
- Ephesians 6:10-20
- Philippians 3
- 1 Timothy 6:11-19
- 1 Peter 1:13-2: 3